ALLEN MASTON

REKINDLE

THE RALLYING OF A GENERATION BACK TO GOD

Thank you

To my Lord and Savior Jesus Christ. I love you. Humbly. I would be, and am nothing without you. Why you would ever pick me is beyond me. A special thanks to all who have helped with this project (there are so many of you). And to my mother, Candance Camphor McLemore - "Made it Ma! Top of the world!"

CONTENT

FOREWORD

My brother was in the in the ministry long before I was and with this book proves that although one may not be seen it does not mean that one is not with God. his passion for the word and for the things of the kingdom are evident. Allen's book is full of what I would call theological goodies,It is honest and heartfelt a deep dig that puts me in mind of C.S. Lewis Mere Christianity or even The Screwtape letters . This book holds truths which cause you to pause and ponder. It is not one that can [or should] beread in a hurry. while artistic, daunting and theoretic it has a most urgent message that pulls the reader in with its insight on being rekindled to the Father's heart. The greatest moments in the book are the visions that he unfolds like pictures. This book calls the reader to come up higher, dig deeper and explore the beauty of God for themselves. There is also his unmistakable love for theatre, written art, and film of which I share and sense of humour that clearly channels our mother saying things like

The devil is a liar, and is his mother-in-law, The way you feel has nothing to do with the price of tea in China and so on I recommend you read but prepare for this thesis to challenge your thinking, God is not dead, but indeed alive in each one of us, we just have to ignite the fire that was called to burn in us before the foundation of the earth. Congratulations Allen on answering the Call of God.

Dr. Alexis Maston-Mcclinton

RALLYING A GENERATION TOO GOD
A COMMENTARY

In today's world, everyone seemingly has a voice that in their minds they feel they have something of value to say…but its' based solely on their own truth. This social on slot of activity has created a situation where many factions have entered and infiltrated the church, and even has taken the position of acting as though they are indeed the church. These factions who are very deceptive and whose motive is specifically to mount a mass separation and departure among church goers from the truth.

Where is God? Is the hearts cry of many who have witnessed the demise of the church as the reputation of Christ is battered with evil works and false representations by perpetrators who seek to destroy the true church.

Well I am here to tell you that we are not having it. No longer will this charade be allowed to take the place of Christ. STOP IT NOW, is the heart cry being echoed across America and throughout the world, as a powerful remnant take their strategic positions to recapture territory that belongs to the church which is Christ.

In this auspicious work inscribed by author Allen Maston, it is certainly pointed rightly to strike the heart of those who will hear, listen and do what is required to rally an awakening of what is truth, thereby inspiring a true revolution to a true revival. The RESET is inevitable and Allen Maston's book is the bow that will fire the arrow into a waiting world of truth seekers, and many in this generation will come to God through this master piece of truth.

Reactivate Empower Stimulate Exact Truth

Commentary by Pastor Gary L. Wilkerson Calling Down Heaven Ministries

INTRODUCTION

"Teach me, and I will hold my tongue; Cause me to understand wherein I have erred." (Job 6:24 KJV)

"Let us examine and probe our ways and let us return to the Lord." (Lamentations 3:40 NKJV)

This writing is directed toward the body of Christ—the Church. It is intended to drive the *ecclesia* back to her first love (See Revelation 2:1-7). If you have picked up this book with hopes of philosophical railings against God, you will be disappointed, but you won't be alone. There will be many in the body of Christ who will be equally as disappointed in this book. This is to be expected. The brazen laver can be one of the hardest things to look into because it means one must acknowledge one's <u>own</u> sin and shortcomings. This book was planted in my heart about five years ago, after watching a video by Dr. Ravi Zachariah. A quote he used stood out to me (for a full reading of the madman available in appendix A).

"God is dead. God remains dead. And we have killed him. How shall we comfort ourselves, the murderers of all murderers? What was holiest and mightiest of all that the world has yet known has bled to death under our knives: who will wipe this blood off us? What water is there for us to clean ourselves? What festivals of atonement, what sacred games shall we have to invent? Is not the greatness of this deed too great for us? Must we ourselves not become gods simply to appear worthy of it?"—Nietzsche, The Madman from *The Gay Science*, 125 (see appendix for full parable).

That quote stayed at the back of my mind until one day; the Lord asked me, "Am I dead to you?" After much self-searching, I had to admit to my shame, yes. He had been dead to me for years. This was a great weight. He then revealed and showed me that this wasn't just an Allen Maston problem, though, many people are experiencing this dilemma as well. This issue needs to be addressed in the body of Christ as a whole.

I would like to stress that while this book may read at some points as philosophy, it is not. I don't know much about philosophy, but I do know Scripture. It clearly says to us, *"Don't let anyone capture you with empty philosophies and high-sounding nonsense that come from human thinking or from the spiritual powers of this world, rather than from Christ."* (Colossians 2:8 & Hebrews 13:9). Although I have mentored youth, done world missions, prophesied, and taught in many fields worldwide, I still see myself as a layman. *"The precious Holy Spirit, whom the Father has sent in*

Christ's name, teaches us all things and brings all things to our remembrance. Glory to the true and living God. " (John 14:16 and Nehemiah 9:20). I will flow into various areas when and where the Holy Spirit presses on me heavily, but do not allow this to distract you, as it will all rally together in the end. The goal here is not to attack any individual, denomination, country, or nation. While I will make some comments concerning some things and individuals, I have left the names out with one exception. This is, after all, about the body of Christ as a whole. When you have undertaken a project such as this, your passions can get in the way, leading to ramblings and missed points. This project has, therefore, been undertaken with much prayer and fasting and has been extensively reviewed. With that being said, if you find any theological or doctrinal errors, I ask for your forgiveness. If it is something you simply disagree with, I implore you to search the Scriptures. I sought to write as the Holy Spirit led me, and having known what the Spirit of the Lord has spoken into my heart *via* the Scriptures.

Let's take a real look at the Church's current condition; the bride (universally and individually). We have been cutting the top off of weeds for too long, chopping down trees and leaving the stumps. But our great husbandman really wants to go deeper, and uproot many things; seen and unseen. The Lord desires the unity of His body. Must we not then set aside all silly differences and come to the full knowledge of the Son of God? Having in Him all things therefore in common, let us grow in spiritual maturity unto the full measure and stature of Christ, confessing our sins one to another, exposing the things that have long been buried underneath the surface. Let us cast aside those pesky issues that constantly pop up every generation and regress the development and progression of the Church. If the walls to the city have come down, and if there is no one to rebuild them, where will the people go?

MY PRAYER

Father, from you alone, extends great grace and mercy. I yield myself to you, and the word of knowledge and wisdom that flows from your throne. I ask that you use these words to bring your people back to your heart. Whatever way, or manner that we may have separated ourselves from You, iron out the wrinkles of every vessel and remove any spots. Lord, resurrect Your word in us. Cleanse and wash away every sin, iniquity and transgression that You, Lord, may return for a bride without blemish. Only You can unite the seven, in Jesus' name. AMEN.

Chapter 1

GOD IS DEAD

12 be careful that you do not forget the LORD, who brought you out of Egypt, out of the land of slavery. (Deuteronomy 6:12)

God's not dead, He's surely alive: NewsBoys.

God is dead. Although Nietzsche did not come up with the idea, he did popularize it. You can call Nietzsche's "Madman," a parable used to present this idea of the dead God. It follows the story of a madman. But why is he mad? Many see Nietzsche as a prophet of sorts. Having not read any of his other writings, I must say I know very little about him. I am, however, quite strict about what I label as prophetic. It does not take a prophet to tell you that fire is hot. You only need to get close enough to feel its heat. Prophet or not, the verbiage is set in a prophetic tone. "I have come too early," he says. Perhaps he saw himself as the madman? I know I see myself as him as I write. I echo the madman's call, running into the Church screaming, "Where is God?"

How many of us have said this ourselves, whether in the public square or in the Church as this madman did at the end of the parable. Perhaps, it's because he is indeed looking for God in the public square where He is rarely found. How he was laughed to scorn by those who watched and mocked him. "Where has He gone?" asked one. "Is He on vacation?" asked another. As he leaps in the middle of them, the madman yells, "I seek God." I see a sinking heart when he says, "We have killed him."

While Nietzsche wrote this, he spoke about how the rise of Atheism has killed God and even the idea of Him. I, however, wish to approach this strictly from a Christian perspective. While whatever Nietzsche truly meant has probably given people headache. We cannot deny that this is extremely important to the Church. But not because the world thinks and acts as if God is dead. This parable is 130 years old. Take a look at the statement and really ponder over it. "Is God is dead?"

In general, as far as the world is concerned, He has always been dead since the fall of man. Except for a few nations, God has always been dead to us. The madman does something curious that I believe most Christians are guilty of—he asserts God's existence, assumes His omnipotence, but at the same time gives a glaring contradiction, saying, "Gods too, can decompose," placing *YHVH (the One true*

God) in the same league as idols: Zeus, Hercules, Odin, or Buddha, which are not gods, but humans that have been deified—idols made of hands. *Shall a man make gods unto himself, and they are no gods?* (Jeremiah 16:20).

The gods of old have all died. And we, the Church, are better for it. But humanity will never be given to idolatry and the desire to usurp God's throne. There will always be those who will say that they are Him, but in the end, it is death. One of these men was named Jose Louis de Jesus, a cult leader. He gathered a huge following of people claiming that he was the second coming of Jesus Christ; he died on August 8, 2013.

I heard of another young man who travels around America patterning himself after Benny Hinn, and his followers are more than happy to go on social media and proclaim that he is literally—Jesus. He has yet to correct them of this blasphemy. This man and those who follow him must repent, or they will perish as well. And there are many others.

What's interesting is that Jesus Christ tells us this is exactly what will happen. *"For many will come in My name [misusing it and appropriating the strength of the name which belongs to Me], saying, 'I am the Christ (the Messiah, the Anointed),' and they will mislead many"* (Matthew 24:5 amp). Unfortunately, people are still being greatly deceived and flocking to these individuals who claim to be Christ.

Deception or not, the question is still sound as God asked

me, "Am I Dead?" And if so, how does one kill the actual God? The madman pondered over this question when he asked, "But how did we do this? How could we drink up the sea? Who gave us the sponge to wipe away the entire horizon? What were we doing when we unchained this earth from its sun?"

NATURAL LAW

Decay is a universal law. It's inevitable that everything eventually falls apart, ages, and wears out. Even death is a manifestation of this law, ashes to ashes, dust to dust. This second law of thermodynamics sounds a lot like, *"In the sweat of thy face shalt thou eat bread, till thou return unto the ground; for out of it wast thou taken: for dust thou art, and unto dust shalt thou return"* (Genesis 3:19 KJV).

Every man, woman, and child born on this earth will pass away one day. Every plant, animal, and living creature will eventually die, even the lifespan of the sun, the moon, and the stars are winding down like an old pocket watch. "Truly, everything that has a beginning has an end"

So, let us take the throne for ourselves. Yes, after all, GOD is dead. Gods can die. What a coup. To the non-believer, it is a fair concept to accept. They don't believe that God exists anyway. However, what they really mean is that they have no confidence in Him. *For it is the fool who says in his heart there is no God, and we know without faith, it is impossible to please God* (Hebrew 11:6). But since this isn't directed to non-believers, this is another subject for another time.

I have heard it said, "If you can make God bleed, then people will cease to believe in Him and there will be blood in the water and the sharks will come." Is this not what the madman had declared when he said, "What was holiest and mightiest of all that the world has yet owned, has bled to death under our knives. Who will wipe this blood off us? What water is there for us to clean ourselves?" It is intriguing to me that Nietzsche uses the images of blood and asks, who will clean us? The blood of Jesus cannot be wiped off once applied. Also, only His blood can clean and redeem us in this, Selah.

I do, however, agree with Nietzsche—damage occurred from our knives. But to what has the damage been done, you might ask? Well… to God's reputation. But by whom? Don't worry; we'll get there. By this type of damage, statements like *God is Dead* are raised.

WELL, WHY CAN'T YOUR GOD DIE?

His name is I AM. His beginning is continual and infinitum, as is His end. He is both first and last. He is the One true and living God. He is uncreated. He is neither plant nor animal. He is not a man or mankind, nor is He created by man (as if man could create something out of nothing). He is not the universe, nor is He affected by it. He (*Jehovah God*) who exists outside of time, space, and matter. For *"In the beginning [before all time] was the word (Christ), and the word was with God, and the word was God Himself"* (John 1:1 AMP). To put a very fine point on it "He" is. Thus, He cannot die.

To create time, space, and matter, He must be above them, beyond them, or He is not God. He is the only being whose reason for existing is solely within Himself. He is the first uncaused cause. [He] says this about Himself at least six times in Scripture (Isaiah 44:6, 48:12, Revelation 1:8, 1:17, 21:6, 22:13). It is written, in the mouth of two or three witnesses shall every word be established (2 Corinthians 13:1 and John 4:24). He is a Spirit. And as such, the laws of the created place do not apply to Him, the Heavenly realm, or the Spirit realm.

ALL THINGS IN HIM

In the beginning, God created everything we see and experience; it all holds its origin with Him. Did the scriptures not declare, *"For by Him were all things created, that are in heaven, and that are in earth, visible and invisible, whether they be thrones, or dominions, or principalities, or powers: all things were created by him, and for him:"* (Colossians 1:16). And in another place, it's stated, *"All things were made by him; and without him was not anything made that was made"* (John 1:3).

He made all things, and there's nothing that He did not create—death included. As Creator over all, His rule is absolute. He holds complete authority over everything and so, is in no way subject to the things He created. This is why death is subject to those who are in Christ Jesus. Therefore, by Christ and through Christ do we testify that we overcome by the blood of the Lamb (which is Jesus Christ) and the word of our testimony.

Despite all this—God is Dead? Our God, the Creator of the universe itself, is dead? Yes, and we have killed Him. Look at the state of the Church and tell me that God has not died under our boot heels, and at the edge of our knives. As the nations did to the prophets, or the Pharisees in ancient Rome, driving Pilate to crucify what was *holiest* on earth. I believe that, in many ways, we as the Church have made the true and living God bleed or, at best, wounded His heart. The word of God tells us that He has emotions and feelings. He has wants and desires, although He is not sustained by these as we are.

Someone may say, "How dare you say the Church is responsible. Thou art a heretic!" But is it really that hard to fathom? Mind you; I do not mean the Church as it is spread out through all time, space, and eternity. That, as Screwtape lamented, is a dreadful sight. It is, however, true. We, His people, have killed Him. According to a 2018 survey, 58 percent of Christians see little need to study Christian creeds and confessions. Ask yourself how often you wake up and realize you haven't read His word or prayed for weeks, or even months, on end. So much for studying to show thyself approved. Oh, but we will swear we study, pray, and seek the Lord. How pretentious we are.

What do you reach for first in the morning? Your phone, a cup of coffee, the remote control, or your lover? We often go a whole day or a week without properly acknowledging the Father. Please, tell me again how He isn't dead to you in some way?

I myself am not out of the woods here by any means. At one point after being asked this question by God, I realized that I hadn't truly prayed or read the word in years. Yes, it had been years. We have to be honest here. Oftentimes, we assume that communing with the Lord means quoting a scripture here or there, listening to Christian radio, wearing a chain with a cross on it, or talking about Him. Tell me if any of your relationships would really last if they were based on the type of sporadic communication you currently have with Him. I'm sure they wouldn't.

At a time I was living in Los Angeles pursuing acting, the Lord said to me, "You don't love Me because you don't know Me. You don't know Me because you don't spend time with Me, and you don't spend time with Me because you don't love Me. And you don't love Me because you don't know Me." Talk about a moment! I'm still chewing on that!!!

Toward the final portion of the "Madman," he is seen going from Church to Church looking for God. There are about 2.18 billion Christians in the world today and about 37 million Christian Churches. Which one did he visit while he lamented, "What, after all, are these Churches now if they are not the tombs and sepulchers of God?"

Jesus put it this way: *"Woe to you, scribes and Pharisees, you hypocrites! You are whitewashed sepulchres, which indeed appear beautiful outwardly, but are full of dead men's, and all uncleanness"* (Matthew 23:27). Have we become what we so adamantly speak against?

We've all heard the phrase, "You are dead to me!" Probably in some dramatic episode of television, usually delivered after someone has been hurt. It is as though the Church has said to God, "You are dead to me." But why? What has He done? What fault have we found in Him that we have strayed so far away from Him? Why is God who is not subject to death—dead to so many who call Him Lord?

CRUCIFY HIM AGAIN

I remember being at a concert by a very popular artist. At the end of the concert, the artist opened the floor for questions and a woman asked very directly, without flinching, "Are you a believer?" This artist, who is a "preacher's kid," whose earliest albums would always have one or two songs about Christ, responded, "I won't get into a religious discussion, but if you're asking me if I believe there's a higher power, yeah. Is that power what I was raised to believe? I don't know. See, I've traveled the world and knowing what I know now, I do believe there is something out there, but I don't know what."

Jesus said, "But whoever disowns me before others, I will disown before my Father in heaven." (Matthew 10:33).

Talk about killing the word. The artist's words were an out-and-out rejection of the word. I was hurt, frustrated, and angry by this. How could you stand up in front of all these people and deny Him like that?

As much as his answer shook me, can I really say I've done no different? I slept with the woman I went to the concert with that night. We weren't married. Sin is sin. So the rejection of the word was still the same. Essentially then, I was saying to Him, *you're dead to* me. Although I have never blatantly denied Him before men with my words. I have denied Him with my actions. Truth be told, I've denied Him more times than Peter... wretched man that I have been.

Praise the Lord for His mercy and grace.

Look back over your life, and ask yourself, "Is God dead to me?" *Is He in His holy temple* (Habakkuk 2:20). *Does His train and word fill it?* (Isaiah 6:1). What about my speech, my habits, my marriage, and my heart? Am I easily yielded to sin? *You are the servant of who you obey* (Romans 6:16). And though our service bounces back and forth, you can only truly serve one (Matthew 6:24).

BIBLICAL DEATH

In the beginning, God created the heavens and the earth and every animal was filled with life… In Hebrew, 'Chay' khah'·ē (Strong's *H2416*) means life; this is the life of the flesh. The same life every animal has, Adam had, but Adam was made in God's image as a *Trinity*— spirit, body, and soul (Genesis 2:7). *For man became a living soul and everything was good* (Genesis 1:31). We were told to eat of every tree in the garden (Genesis 2:16), which includes the tree of life. I'll say that again; we were not restricted from the tree of life, we were told to eat of it. The only tree that was off-limits was the tree of the knowledge of good and evil (Genesis 2:17).

Many have suggested that God was trying to keep us from something, to keep us from being like Him, but this suggestion does not bear out logically because we were already like Him (made in His image). Having created us, His expectation for us to obey does not come from a desire to control but because He loves us. Those of us with children understand that the restrictions we put in place are there to protect. We had already been offered His eternal life.

Why place it there anyway? How can one choose if there are no choices? Questions of predetermination might arise here. To those I offer this statement—if one does not know what is predetermined, one might as well not be.

Adam was made in God's image and likeness but was not "one" with Him, essentially the same way a husband and wife shall become one (Genesis 2:24). My son is like me, in my image, but my wife is one with me. Do you see the difference? This oneness requires a choice to be made between the tree of death and evil or the tree of life and goodness. Choose the *zōē* life (Strong's G2222); be completely one with Him by accepting His Spirit and allowing Him to take up residence within you. Having loved Him and obeyed Him, Adam would then be filled with Him and His eternal uncreated life. As Christ tells us in John 14:23, "Anyone who loves me and obeys My teachings, My Father will love them and We will come take up residence with them." Wow, consider this. Man, a blank canvas of sorts, is given life contingent on his obedience—to accept Him (God) and to be filled with and led by His eternal uncreated life and Spirit, uniting with the *Trinity*. This was always God's goal. We know what happened. The man and his wife both ate, thus separating Adam from his Creator (Genesis 3:6). He was filled with, and united with *sin*. Is this not continuously the decision we are faced with, choosing Jesus Christ, the God of life (the *zōē* life) or choosing sin, choosing Lucifer, and the life of the flesh?

YOU SHALL SURELY DIE

"But of the tree of the knowledge of good and evil, thou shalt not eat of it: for in the day that thou eatest thereof thou shalt surely die" (Genesis 2:17).

Making a choice and being separated from the word (Jesus) who was in the beginning with God and was God, caused us to die. This is the first time the word die appears in the Scripture. But what does *die* mean? Mr. Webster tells us it is when a person, animal, or plant stops living (so, a fleshly death). This is true in a sense because anything disconnected from its source will ultimately die. The word here holds a slightly different meaning. In Hebrew, the word is MUWTH {müth} (Strong's H4191): to die, kill, have one executed (as a penalty), be put to death, to die prematurely (by the neglect of wise moral conduct).

Therefore, we see the death that occurred after the fall was a penalty, a punishment because of disobedience. Consider this also—the penalty of this separation and death had only been handed down once before to Lucifer after his rejection and rebellion against God. Uniting with Lucifer and sin unites us with his punishment of eternal death. It is sin that does the works, and it is sin that receives the payment along with anything connected to sin. Doing the works of sin (Romans 6:23). For Adam, the image of God within us was part of this death. The soul and spirit of man separated from God's Spirit (John 4:24).

Why, then, does man still live? When 164,383 people die a day. Tell me, does man really live? Here, Mr. Webster's end of life definition comes into play. Although the spirit died, God created man: Adam (male and female), a body and a living soul just like any other animal (Genesis 2:7). The Scripture tells us that the spirit returns to God from where it came and the body to the earth, and the soul goes either to heaven or hell (Ecclesiastes 12:7). That soul and the flesh are tied together through blood. The life of the flesh is in the blood (Leviticus 17:11, and again in Genesis 9:4). Part of the dietary law is to not eat anything with blood in it. The word *life* here in Hebrew is the word *nephesh* (Strong's

H5315). Its first meaning is *soul.* Additionally, it also means *self-life, mind, appetite, desire, emotion.* Could this be why the Lord says to Cain, your brother's blood cries out to me from the earth (Genesis 4:10). The soul is therefore confined and found in the blood. .

Scripture tells us that the word can divide asunder the soul and the spirit therefore, the soul and spirit is one (Hebrews 4:12). The priests of old would use a knife to separate the animal on the altar and separate its bones and sinew. The knife had to be perfectly smooth, and free of any nicks, making the cut swift. The word of God is this knife, separating our soul from the spirit of sin. So, part of us that was like God (*the original creation*) died without the word. We are now walking corpses, bound for the resurrection of eternal death (John 5:29). We must be separated from that death and from sin, and only the word is sharp enough to accomplish this.

Consider a wedding. A venue (the earth). The guests are prepared (all creation, angels, and animals). The bride is created (mankind) and brought to the venue, but there are two grooms and two covenant meals; life and good, death and evil. The meal, thus eaten, was death and evil. The bride is now wed to sin and death—married to it! In fact, in covenant with it! Only divorce can destroy this covenant. Enter the word of God, the *logos* that is sharper than any two-edged sword (Hebrews 4:12).

BORN OF THE FLESH

Jesus tells us that what is born of the flesh is flesh. *What is born of the Spirit is spirit* (John 3:6). People tend to jump from one relationship to another. God's not having that. God is calling us to join Him and remain with Him in setting ourselves apart from sin. *For we are labourers with Him* (1 Corinthians 3:9). Having been tainted by its covenant with sin, the flesh must be resurrected to be fit for its new bridegroom. Repairing and reforming the flesh is impossible. *God cannot dwell where there is sin* (Psalm 5:4). He will make the flesh new through resurrection. The spirit of man is made new in Christ Jesus. He (Christ, the word) is the resurrection and the life, as He said to Mary in (John 17:14). *We must die to sin* (Romans 6:11, and be resurrected in Him). This does not mean we should wait until the flesh is physically dead but to be made new and united with Him now. We count ourselves as dead. United through this new covenant through Jesus, the bride is bound to obey His word. *For what bride does not obey the word of her husband* (Ephesians 5:22-24).

A TERRIBLE SWORD

This two-edged sword also points us to the raw harsh truth of the Living word. Jesus is the great physician (Mark 2:15-17). Like a surgeon, He is about to cut something out, "Piercing even to the dividing asunder of soul and spirit." Jesus can separate who we are as a spirit and what we are as fallen men (Romans 12:2). Now that you are new, do not conform to the law or word of the world but renew your mind to the *logos,* the true word.

God would not want to separate us from His Spirit, particularly after it took so much work to get us connected. Oh, the wonder that is the Cross. What is easier? (Matthew 9:5 and Luke 5:23) tell us creation is easy; death is easy—redemption is hard. His word is designed to separate us from the spirit of sin. Thus separated, we can begin to renew our minds and not be conformed to this world. Again, being reformed by the word from His mouth (Revelation 19:15), is it not a terrible swift sword (Isaiah 27:1) unmatched in creative and distinctive power? Glory to the Lamb.

When you look at the outline of biblical death, in short, it is the eternal mental, physical, and spiritual separation of man from the Lord God, the Creator of all, and the binding of him to sin and death. We see how and why we die, and that God cannot die. We see that it is the word of God that has died in us, in the Church, and in our individual lives.

KILL THE WORD, KILL THE KING

The cunning warrior attacks neither body nor mind. First, he attacks his heart! The Father loves the Son, the word (John 3:35, John 5:20, and 2 Peter 1:17). God says He places His word above His name (Psalm 138:2). *The Son is in the bosom of the Father* (John 1:18). As with any father, to attack His heart, then, is to attack His Son, His word. Kill the word, and you kill the king! This is about ruining God's word and His character. That's what it's always been about from the gate; that's always been the plan—question the word. In 2 Corinthians, Paul lamented: I am afraid that just as Eve was deceived by the serpent's cunning and twisted words, your minds may somehow be led astray from your sincere and pure devotion to Christ. How was Eve deceived? By changing the word. When asked if God had said a certain thing, she added to the word, saying, "God said we shall not eat or touch it." So, the snake knows she is willing to change the word. But all she did was add a restriction; how can that be bad? But Deuteronomy 12:32 teaches us do not add or subtract.

The Scripture says a good name is rather to be chosen than great riches, and loving favour rather than silver and gold. What name is better than His? God's name is good; it's great; it is the name above every name (Philippians 2:9); and it's a strong tower (Psalm 18:10). *But no one has seen Him* (John 1:8). It is the Son, the word, that declares Him. So, this is the smart, cunning attack. Kill the word; make His name no good so no one will trust Him. This would be the best place to cause destruction. His honour, His name, and His word are as connected as our soul is to our flesh. His word is the foundation for everything, and nothing was made without it. That's the foundation of the universe—GOD'S word. Is this not why He was sent to be tempted by the enemy in the wilderness (Matthew 4:1-11), in an all-out attempt to completely destroy the word? Here again, the second Adam is given the choice the first Adam was. What choice? To be dishonorable. To deny His word. It's curious that the enemy brings into question what the Father had already said and promised Him. let's take an ear to the conversation (authors rendition of Christ's temptations):

"Turn these stones into bread."

"Nope, man shall not live by bread alone, and, besides, I am the bread of life."

"Cast yourself down and the angels will take you up."

"Nope, you will not tempt the Lord your God."

"I will give you every kingdom of the world if you bow to me."

To this, Jesus says, "Get behind me; love the Lord your God and him only shall you serve."

Jesus had already been promised all the nations of the earth as His inheritance (Isaiah 49:6).

So what exactly could the enemy offer Him? Nothing.

I love how Jesus—the Word—used the word of God to destroy the twisted works and lies of the devil (1 John 1:8). So why then do we as the body of Christ not feast on the bread of life (which is the word of God)? Did Jesus not say, "Lest you eat my body, you have no part in me" (John 6:53). We must apply the word of God and declare it in our daily lives.

GUILTY BY ASSOCIATION

If your name is bad, no one wants to even associate with you. We don't like to hang out with the person who has a bad name. Don't hang out with those people, your mother used to say. They're no-good ragamuffins. No one wants to be guilty by association (judged by the company that you keep). However, good or bad, we are all judged by that company. The principle, evil communication corrupts good manners (1 Corinthians 15:33) is being put into play here. If the wicked one can kill the word, God's name goes bad and no one wants to hang out with Him. For example I have heard it said, "Healing, prophecy, miracles?" He doesn't do those things anymore". If these things don't occur where you fellowship, could it be that the word is dead in that area?

I recently read about a pastor being asked to pray that a woman's child be raised from the dead. The pastor obliged her request, a clear word-based action. For they will do these works and greater works shall they also do (John 4:12, Mark 11:23, and Matthew 10:8). Time would fail me to list miracles such as these that have happened in our time.

Consider. At a tent meeting in Birmingham, Alabama, on March 22, 1959, a child David H., received 26 miracles in one night. The mother attended the tent meeting for a week, and her son was not yet healed. The morning before the healing took place; she asked a young RW Schambach when her son would be healed, fearing they would leave without the healing. He said, "I will not make excuses for what the Holy Spirit does or doesn't do." The young boy was healed of 26 birth defects and diseases (see miracle magazine—May 1959; volume 4, No.8).

Why was the pastor ridiculed, berated, and taken through the wringer for praying that this woman's child is raised from the dead? For standing on the word? Well, was the child raised from the dead or not? No, but that's not the issue. The issue is belief and faith in the word, no matter what. Anyone unwilling to stand on the word has no confidence in it. People will disassociate with the word or make excuses for the word not working. Either the word of God is, or it isn't. Is He a healer, a deliverer, or is He not? He is either a waymaker, a miracle worker, or isn't? Either God is or He isn't. Whether raised in this life or the next, the child is raised.

See how the enemy's cunning devices bring division and separation, even among the body of Christ? Note the lack of understanding and lack of communication. We run from godly unity and relish separation. The Church is divided with (by my count) 208 different versions of Scripture, Eastern and Western theology, Catholicism, Protestantism, Eastern Orthodoxy, Anglicanism, Oriental Orthodoxy, and the Assyrians. The skeptic screams, "You can't even agree on what you believe." Beloved, the Father, the Word (Yeshua), and the Holy Ghost all agree, and these three are ONE (1 John 5:7). Why aren't we?

But your education and denomination say that you know the word. No, you understand it with your intellectual faculties. Tell me, can the wisdom that comes from the knowledge of the flesh (good and evil), which God demands be destroyed, assist man in knowing the word of God?

Sometimes we cannot conjure up a logical reason for why we disagree with something; sometimes, we cannot articulate why we disagree with it, but in the Spirit, we know it's wrong.

Other times, we completely agree with something because it makes all the sense in the world. We can prove it logically and historically, but over time, the Holy Spirit will tell us this is not the way, and later we will understand why.

To truly know the Living word, by definition, means you have developed a relationship with the one who breathed it through meeting and spending time with Him; you're familiar and friendly with Him. This is done with the Spirit, for His words are spirit and life. Thus, understanding or being aware of something through observation, inquiry, or information is done with intellect. The spiritual man who is led by the Spirit of God, therefore, knows the word, as he is led by the Spirit and not by understanding with the mind. With the Spirit, we know and believe. Paul did not seek anyone's instruction after being saved; he went straight to Arabia and received instruction from the Lord—the word (Galatians 1:17).

If we must pour over many theological references and compare, observe, and search with the natural mind until we come to know the truth of the word, then only those with higher education and strong minds will know and understand His truth.

The Greeks took pride in their logic; indeed, we still teach their logic today. The Pharisees and Sadducees were teachers of the law, deeply steeped in it. But unto the Greeks, the preaching of the Cross was foolishness and unto the Jews a stumbling block.

Is this not why Paul said in Philippians 3:8, *"I count everything I know as dung for the knowledge of Christ."* Let us therefore lean not unto our own understanding. Desiring to be wise in our own eyes has he not used the foolish things of the world to confound the wise and use what was not to bring to nought what is. (1 Corinthians 1:28).

Could it be that in each of these "Churches" (I use the term loosely), we give the illusion that we are ever in and know His word, giving ourselves to the study of it (Acts 17:11, 1 Timothy 2:15), living off it as workmen needing not to be ashamed? Here is the truth—we have refused to keep it, study it, or read it. We refuse to let it sustain us. Seriously, when was the last time you actually read Revelation? We have made it of little effect (Matthew 7:13). And so the Father is judged, and His honor is brought into question by those outside the faith due to the actions of those in it. Every time my wife and I go somewhere and I look a bit disheveled; she always says, "You represent me." As a part of His glory, we represent Him, and He is, in turn, judged by that representation.

Chapter 2

STRONG AS EVER

MURDERERS OF ALL MURDERERS

We have killed His word. We have lied on Him. We don't believe in His word (no, not *entirely*). We don't read it. We don't quote it. We don't trust *and* rely confidently on His word with ALL of our hearts. Instead, some rely on their insight and understanding (Proverbs 3:5-6), and for others, it's fear of perception, fear of how they will be seen not only in the public square but in the Church.

As is always the case after we reject the word, we can't hear from God and we run to the universe and false gods. We run to the witch of Endor like Saul did (Samuel 28). We have let it fall away into hallowed halls, turning them into tombs of His eternal life. By not keeping His word before us, we have buried it by not walking in His statutes or holding ourselves and our leaders to His standard. We are not contending for the faith, giving cookie-cutter services and turning ministry into marketing... offering worship not fit for a King. Three fast songs, two slow. Everyone's a superstar pastor or a YouTube prophet, quoting psychics "I received a word."— Stop it.

We have killed His word and therefore, have killed Him. Yes, not as humanity as a whole, not atheism or pantheism, but we as the body of Christ through our actions or/and inactions, we who claim to represent Him. We have slain that which is most *Holy.* We have been like cancer to the very body we claim to be a part of.

BUT WE DON'T NEED IT

An old saying goes, "The things you read in the Bible, ain't necessarily so." The Bible tells us that miracles happen, that extraordinary things occur. The Exodus, the birth of Jesus to a virgin, His resurrection from the grave, the worldwide flood, and original sin are all foundational to Christians. Our desire to run from the historical truth of the word of God has caused us to run in circles—the blind leading the blind into the Sea of Foolishness.

I spoke with one man at LA Fashion Week 2015 who said, "The Red Sea never parted; they walked over it in the dry season because Moses stood on top of the sphinx and saw that it was low." Any excuse will do, right? Apparently, anything that says God's word was only for Bronze Age individuals and no longer holds any sway in our culture is acceptable no matter how silly it sounds. At some point, we have all heard things like this. From primary school to university, television, cinema, and theater, politics and news—all have been used to convey the idea that the word of God is not relevant for today. And who is this God anyway? Have you ever made this statement? Has it burned in your mind? I know it had in mine.

I ask you to consider this—Jesus is the word of God. To say that the scripture is irrelevant or it was merely written by the hands of man suggests that Christ Himself is irrelevant and merely a creation of man. In an interview, a pastor was asked about the reliability of events in Scripture. He said, "It doesn't matter if these things actually happened—what matters is what they can teach us." We must be very careful here. Incorrect interpretation of scientific evidence does not change the word of God. Archaeological evidence, or the lack thereof, does not change the word of God. Your need to be right, your disappointments, your opinion, your resentments, your regrets, and your desires to sin without consequence does not change the word of God (Matthew 5:18). If we truly want to live our best life now, then we must let this mind be in us that was also in Christ Jesus. God's word is true and every man who disagrees with it is a willful liar. Don't altar the word. *ALL the word is given by the inspiration of God* (2 Timothy 3:15-17).

SAME STUFF, DIFFERENT AGES

As we discussed, we know that God (*Adonai*) is not subject to death. We understand it is we humanity who is dead.

What we are speaking about is the death of His word in us. It's what happens when the word of God is not properly taught, when it is dismissed as a myth or just a good idea, when Christ is made just a consciousness and not the fullness of God, when the *logos* is just one of many options in a cavalcade of deities or an avatar and brother to all other holy men and sages instead of the way, the truth, and the life (John 14:6), who is the only begotten of the Father, who had glory with Him before time began (John 17:5).

It's not the first time we have come to this point in the Church. I would run out of pages to speak about the generations before us who experienced this. In 1651, for example, the Church of Scotland drew up what they called a "Humble Acknowledgment of the Sins of the Ministry." These were clergy, men of the word, and by their own account, their sins were compounded, including "Ignorance of God, lack of nearness with Him, little time spent in reading, meditating, and speaking the word. Exceeding great selfishness in everything, acting from, for and to ourselves. Not caring how unfaithful and negligent others were, but being rather content, if not gloating at their faults because it would make us look better. Rarely in the secret place of praying to God, except to look good in public performance; and even that much neglected, done superficially." They then said they put too little emphasis on God's word.

How did they do that? Well, according to them, by not studying and honoring God's word. Elevating man's writings, opinions, and systems in their studies over the word. Drinking more out of human wisdom than God's. Because of this, their spirits, lives, and words were formed and derived more from man than God. They lamented, "We must study the Bible more, steep our souls in it. We must not only lay it up within us but transfuse it through the whole texture of the soul" (Excerpts taken from a humble acknowledgment of the sins of the ministry in Scotland, by the Church of Scotland 1651).Notice, it was not one clergyman that wrote it but signed by the Church as a whole. Sounds to me like the Church of Scotland in 1651 had the same issues we have—the death of God through the death of the word. Same stuff, different ages.

GOD WILL SEND A MAN

It is interesting to look back through the holy Scriptures and see that the story of the death of the word of God has played itself out there as well. It seems this process is always the same. God creates something. He starts it. He gives it a promise. As things start out all right, lo and behold, someone is disobedient, someone begins to doubt, and someone asks—as the serpent did in the garden—has God really said...? Will God really do…? (Genesis 3:3). When one is not clear on what God's word says, contradiction comes in and sows doubt, and, ultimately, a fall WILL take place.

He (God) then sends a man or woman to be the mediator to bring those changes to restore His people back to His word (Zephaniah 3:20). Mind you; I am not saying by any means that I am that person. I do, however, know that a Josiah-like spirit has risen. And it has hit a generation who has asked, *Where is the power? Where is the promise? Where is the manifested glory of this God you speak of? Is God dead?* No, beloved. His word has been sent to heal us (Psalm 107:20), and to set the body back in order so He can fulfill the work He intended from the very beginning.

THE OLD GOOD ROAD

When people forget the word of the King, they forget the promises He made in His word. Things go bad, things get off track, and people perish from the lack of knowledge (Hosea 4:6). Why do the heathens blaspheme God? Because the people of God have forgotten their God and so they are in bondage... again (Isaiah 52:5). For these reasons and more, you need mediators to remind people of the way things are supposed to be, to show them the path on the old good road once again. As the Scriptures say in Jeremiah 6:16, Thus says the Lord, "Stand by the roads and look; ask for the ancient paths, Where the good way is; then walk in it, and you will find rest for your souls. But they said, "We will not walk in it!"

I was shown this scripture by the Lord about five years ago as I drank coffee. He told me to "go by the old good road" and ask it, "What is the way to go? What is the right path? I have been blessed in the years to have been privileged to know godly men and women who helped me see and stay on the path of God— Jean Maurice Njembelle, Dr. Ron Hale Sr, Dr. Donneta Hale, Pastor Gary Wilkerson, Tim Craig, the late Dr. Sokora Mesa, Margo Shields, my twin sister Dr. Alexis Maston-McClinton and my wonderful wife, Tyree Maston.

Like many others who have been a great influence in my life, I accredit the Lord God for bringing them to me. I often say I am a student of dead men and women. Even the writings and words of people who have been dead for centuries have led me to the old good road.

Many have been shown and have refused it. Many will not walk in it. Many have walked away from it. Many have kept the word buried and are keeping God, in essence, dead. Will we, in this dispensation, do the same?

Chapter 3

THE DAYS MAN

FIVE-FINGER DEATH PUNCH

In 1900 years, the Church has never been in a better position than it is now. The last two ascension gifts (gifts Christ gave as He ascended), Ephesians 4:8, have been rebirthed for the first time in centuries. The offices of the evangelist, apostle, prophet, pastor, and the teachers are all functioning. Now we must unite them as one. Let's strike a blow… Let's Go, Voltron Force! Jesus let us know that these gifts were given for the perfecting of the saints, for the work of the ministry. What is that work? What is that perfecting? Leading us and keeping us on the good old road, keeping us in the word of God until we are united and the full measure, and stature of Christ.

For those who believe in the cessation of the gifts, offices, and their functions, I ask you, is the Church perfected? Are we united as one as He prayed? Aren't new converts coming on board and joining the body every day? Are there not new soldiers being sent out into the battlefield? Why would the Lord Jesus Christ send out the first century Church better equipped than those of us going out now in this day and age? Has spiritual warfare changed? Last I checked, we were still in a battle with the enemy. This battle is not for the faint-hearted or ill-equipped but the fully clad warrior who has been well-trained with the weapons of our warfare, which are not carnal (2 Corinthians 10:4). It makes no spiritual or logical sense to take away those weapons. All soldiers get the same training manuals, materials, and weapons—Selah.

WAGING WAR

I have said, we are like Voltron or maybe even the power rangers and need to unite and strike a blow. The enemy's attack here is to destroy the word, and is it any surprise his whole position is to kill, steal, and destroy (John 10:10). Make no mistake, brothers and sisters, we are fighting a spiritual war. The battle against principalities, powers, the rulers of the darkness of this world, and spiritual wickedness in high places, Ephesians 6:10-12, wages on. So, put on the full armor of God and stand; quench fiery darts with your shield, which is our faith, but our principal weapon in this fight is the word. Don't lose it. This weapon is your life. Christ won the war, but the battle is not yet over. Gird up yourselves as men of war. Take the staff of the Lord, the rod of God (Exodus 4:2).

It is imperative that we are built up, not broken down. Be

humble, but know when to wage war. I have learned a thing or two about the importance of spiritual warfare. Accountability and knowing what Scriptures to use in the time battle is vital. You can't hit the bull's eye if you're not looking at the right target—then what are you aiming at? So, if I could share anything with you, it's this: Warfare takes you through trial and error. You may take a knee, but don't go down. You don't want the enemy to gain ground in your atmosphere or territory. As you learn the tools and weaponry of how to effectively fight back intentionally against the enemy, WAR in the authority God has given you through prayer, fasting… and His word.

THE DAYSMAN

"Neither is there a daysman between us that may lay his hands upon us both." (Job 9:13).

Daysman: an umpire, arbiter or judge.

The word in Hebrew is *yakach* (Strong's H3198): to prove, decide, judge, rebuke, reprove, correct, arbitrator, umpire, referee, one who stands in a judicial capacity between two parties, and decides upon the merits of their arguments or case at law.

Jesus Christ, of course, was and is our eternal daysman, standing between God and man, bartering the lives of humanity back to Himself. Placing His hand on both God and man with His divinity and humanity, able to bridge the gap, to stop the war between heaven and earth, between

God's kingdom and Adam's, Jesus has come to proclaim that the war is over and to offer us peace on earth (Isaiah 11:6 and Luke 2:14). Albeit, the peace is on God's terms, allowing the sinful man to come into agreement with His law (word) and finally unite with the Holy God.

When I was a kid, we used to have people called hall monitors. We were given a nifty little sash and a clipboard and sent out and empowered to maintain order in the school's corridors. We would resolve issues between our classmates and were taught to listen to both sides of the story. We were taught to look for what they called a POVP or point of view problems between students, and do our best to show those perspectives to them. Now that I think about it, it was really advanced psychological profiling and counseling for 4th-graders.

The Lord sees our perspective. David tells us that His mercy endures forever because He knows that we are but flesh (Psalm 78:39). He knows we are subject to the flesh (Psalm 103:14). Jesus, our high priest, can sympathize with our weaknesses because He was tempted in every way that we have been (Hebrews 4:15), but without sin. Now through His word, we must see ourselves from His perspective. His word is the brazen laver that sits outside the *t*abernacle. The **priests** would see themselves in it and could wash their hands and their feet before making a sacrifice. The Living word shows us where we are dirty before Him, and the blood provides us a means to be made clean. It is the magic mirror gate in *The Never-Ending Story,* showing us our true selves. Will you run away screaming?

Many of our leaders have not spoken for God properly. They have dismissed the word of God, traded it in for making the parishioners feel better or, worse, to keep people in the seats while Jesus pleads our case, making intercession for us before the throne of God (Romans 8:3-4). Is there any wonder that the free flow of power to the body of Christ, in particular, seems to have dried up? Where are the miraculous wonders of the first-century Church—Saint Patrick, RW Schambach, Catherine Kuhlman, AA Allen, and the likes? Where has the power gone? It has died because we let it die.

When the word of God is cheapened and made into an option or a choice, the power we read about and the promises of God we hear about do not seem to manifest. Could it be because the word of God is not allowed to live in our hearts? Does it prove the lack of true power manifesting in our personal lives and the Church as a whole is because we have forgotten the word? Has it been hidden from us or buried after years of entrenched leadership, false prophecies, shoddy revelation, and generations of building altars to other gods? Has the Church become so convoluted that some things which we think are accurate are not actually in His word?

How many pastors and ministers do you know who don't even open their Bibles to teach and yet claim to speak for Christ. Thirty-three percent of the New Testament is direct quotes of or allusions to the Old Testament—that's

7967 verses. The apostles clearly thought the word was important. One Church in Florida merges itself with witchcraft, and the woman actually got up and said that witchcraft and Christianity are compatible. Did you know there is a Covenant of Christian Witches? They have a Mystery School. This actually exists. The devil is a liar and so is his mother-in-law! I tell you, they'll have their reward. If you sit under one of these men or women, or maybe you are one of them, I beseech you, please repent and turn back to your first love in Christ Jesus. You still have time. Too long have our homes been filled with expensive bibles, sitting on bookshelves, gathering dust. Too long has the word lain quiet in the hearts of the Church covered by emotional issues.

This generation must rise as the manifestation of that daysman, to connect the generations before us and after us, back to the word… back to the King. The power of the Holy Spirit is awaiting to manifest himself, to heal these issues, to knock down idols, to remove high places and to remove the clutter. Beneath it, we will find the word of God.

HIS THRONE OR NO THRONE

Many of us want to place the Lord on any old throne, but He will not sit on something that has been sat on by wickedness. He will not sit on a stranger's throne. Not only must we remove the idol, but we must remove the seat it was sitting on and its foundations. Tear it down. Tear it all down! For His throne is established on justice and righteousness (Psalm 89:14). Idols in the body and in our lives have caused the word of God to be lost and dead in our lives. But bless God that His word does not return to Him void (Isaiah 55:11). He has spoken a prophecy over His people and His Church. It will be without spot or wrinkle (Ephesians 5:27). He will present it to Himself beautiful and whole. He will establish His throne in their hearts and sit upon it.

Consider a spirit that comes back and if it finds the house swept clean, but the master is not there, it will go and get seven more wicked than itself (Matthew 12:45). This is an occupation. Here is an idea–just bring down the house and stop it for good! You can't occupy what is not there. The Lord will build a new one. After all, unless the Lord builds it, you labor in vain (Psalm 127:1). Praise God for His word!

JOSIAH

Josiah, king of Judah, was one of these Daysmen. He was of the house of David, and a type or shadow of Christ. We will start this rousing tale as God so frequently does, with a prophecy.

Don't you just love how the Lord steps into the middle of a situation and says what He will do? You just step back and watch how it plays out. His word says it will not return to Him void but will do what He has sent it to do (Isaiah

55:11). Before I began writing this book, the Lord told me that He would establish His throne in my heart and sit upon it. As I write these words, four years have passed and He has done just that. He removed idols that caused the death of the word in my life. He breathed life into my faith, revealing His word, His will, and His way in me, knocking down high places, tearing down thrones, generational curses, strongholds, and other mess I had built up in my life.

Let's take a look at the prophecy of Josiah in 1 Kings 13:1-4:

And, behold, there came a man of God out of Judah by the word of the Lord unto Bethel: and Jeroboam stood by the altar to burn incense. And he cried against the altar in the word of the Lord, and said, O altar, altar, thus saith the Lord; Behold, a child shall be born unto the house of David, Josiah by name; and upon thee shall he offer the priests of the high places that burn incense upon thee, and men's bones shall be burnt upon thee.

Wow, there is so much in this! I scarcely know where to begin, but let's start with the name Josiah.

Josiah: Yo'shiyah: "whom Jehovah heals" (Strong's H2977)

The wonderful thing about Hebrew words, and the Hebrew language as a whole, is that the words define a thing by what it does, so verse 2 could literally read:

> *"Altar, a child will be born of the House of David and his name will be whom Adonai heals."*

I know the Lord wants to heal His Church, His bride, and make her whole without spot or wrinkle.

It's curious to see that the Lord sent an unknown, unnamed prophet to the very place where Jeroboam was set to burn incense to an idol. Obviously, test every spirit by the Spirit, but don't be so quick to knock a parking lot prophecy. All throughout the Scripture, we have prophets coming from somewhere—just showing up, being used by the Lord, and then leaving. They've come to speak a word to not only that altar, but to every altar that had been and/or would be built.

This prophet was sent because king Jeroboam was breaking the first two commandments at once. We find this in Exodus 20:1-6:

> *And God spoke all these words, saying, I am the Lord thy God, which have brought thee out of the land of Egypt, out of the house of bondage. Thou shalt have no other gods before me. Thou shalt not make unto thee any graven image, or any likeness of anything that is in heaven above, or that is in the earth beneath, or that is in the water under the earth. Thou shalt not bow down thyself to them, nor serve them: for I the Lord thy God am a jealous God, visiting the iniquity of the fathers upon the children unto the third and fourth generation of them that hate me; And shewing mercy unto thousands of them that love me, and keep my commandments.*

Look at that. The very thing King Jeroboam was doing as the prophet spoke to the altar and cursed it—acting as if the God of Israel was dead, treating His word as nothing. We must remember the strong oral tradition of the culture in those days. Although there were scrolls of the law, it was also memorized and quoted in homes over the supper table. But let's go deeper than that. The law of kings written by the prophet Samuel, mentioned in 1 Samuel 10:35, tells us clearly the responsibilities of a king. He must write his own Torah scroll, in addition to the one his ancestors left him. The Sanhedrin (71 elders) would then confirm the king's work by comparing it to the Torah scroll in the temple courtyard.

If his ancestors did not leave him a Torah scroll, or if it was lost or damaged, the king must write two scrolls, placing one in his treasury and keeping the second with him at all times, except when in a place where it's not fit to read. His scroll should be with him everywhere he goes—when he goes to war and returns from war; when he sits in judgment, it should be in his lap; when he dies, it should be placed across him. It should always be with him and be read all the days of his life so he would learn to fear *Adonai,* His God, to keep all the words of the *Torah* and His statutes (Deuteronomy 17;19-20). So, it's obvious that Jeroboam knew what he was doing. There was no excuse for burning incense on an altar built for an idol.

Ask yourself. Do you keep His word? Is it with you at all times? I know I keep saying this in different ways, but it's important. If we look at the Church today, can we see how we mirror this? You may say, "But that is the law of kings." That's no excuse. Are we not kings and priests? (Revelation

1:6). And while the law of kings may not apply to us exactly, we are the keepers of a more excellent covenant, having the Holy Spirit, His word being written on our hearts. Should we not therefore, be successful in keeping His law, His word that He places above His name?

> *I will bow down [in worship] toward Your holy temple And give thanks to Your name for Your lovingkindness and Your truth; For You have magnified Your word together with Your name* (Psalm 138:2 AMP)

IDOLS COME EASY, BUT GO HARD

Let's keep looking at 1 Kings 13:2

> *And he cried against the altar in the word of the Lord, and said, O altar, altar, thus saith the Lord; Behold, a child shall be born unto the house of David, Josiah by name; and upon thee shall he offer the priests of the high places that burn incense upon thee, and men's bones shall be burnt upon thee.*

Woah, wait a tick. Did he cry out against the altar? It can be assumed that He laid His hand on it and shouted, but that's not what I see here. I see Him looking at it and shouting at it, "Yo altar. Thus says the word of the Lord, 'You're going down.' Kind of like how David shouted to Goliath, "The Lord will deliver you into my hands." Life and death are in the power of the tongue (Proverbs 18:21). *It is a small member* (James 3:4), but words have power—not just natural power, but spiritual power. For we speak those things that be not as if they were. We say to the mountain be removed and it is (Mark 11:23 and Romans 4:17).

The most common sin we're told to avoid in all of scripture is idolatry. It breaks the first commandment. Adam broke it. I've broken it. You've broken it. Jeroboam broke it. Can we look into the condition of the Church today, and say idols exist? How about idols in our lives or in our hearts. As individuals, of course, we can. John Calvin said that, "Our heart is an idol factory." A factory? Imagine a whole assembly line inside your heart, just making idols. Henry Ford was famous for developing a better, faster way to build a car. Are we not coming up with better ways to create idols every day? Is it any wonder we are told to guard ourselves from idols? (1 John 5:21).

God will not live with the idols we yield to instead of Him. The Holy Spirit will be grieved and will keep quiet. The word will not dwell among idols. He will not join Himself with sin. He will not share His throne or His glory.

> *For thou art not a God that hath pleasure in wickedness: neither shall evil dwell with thee* (Psalm 5:4).

As He has said so frequently, feel free to keep your idols. Seek them for your healing, your blessings, your nation, and your children. Go pray to them if they are so powerful. I do not delight in lifted hands that are dripping with blood and the scent of things offered to idol worship, new moons, and festivals. Even the good that they do is not of Me, because it is not ordained of Me. Workers of iniquity offering up strange fire. I tell you, they have their reward. Pastors, apostles, teachers, and ministers of the gospel hear the word of the Lord. Paul's spirit was TROUBLED within him when he saw that the city was full of idols (Acts 17:16).

The Spirit says, Ichabod, we are full of idols and the Lord has departed (1 Samuel 4:21). Seeing the body in this state, trapped in idolatry, should inspire compassion but also a righteous indignation to contend for the faith within the faith. Even as the law of return was signed in 1950, I am calling you back to Jerusalem. Oh Judah, I am calling you back for the idols are coming down. Why do you think the city had to be destroyed? It was full of idolatry and the word was nowhere to be found (1 Samuel 3:1). Everyone did what was right in their own eyes. But there has come a generation who I desire to be like the prophet out of the west, those that have not bowed their knees to *Baal*. They will declare, the downfall of the idols will come to pass. Not only will they cast down the high places, the altars, the idols but they will destroy the priests who offer incense upon the very altars they worship. Those who have ears to hear, let them hear the word of the Lord. Those who have bowed their knees to these idols, who have burned incense upon the high places, do not take heed to them, nor follow their ways, for they have sold what is *Holy*. The Arc of the Covenant into the temple of *Dagon, but it* will be brought low with their altars. I tell you, their hands and heads will be cut off, and only stumps will remain. I tell you again; they have their reward.

The Lord promised that He would heal His people. He would heal the land that He called His own. He would send one to cast down the *high places* and destroy the idols. Have you or your family known such idols? Does it seem like the word of the Lord has died? Fear not, the spirit of Josiah is coming and will be used in a mighty way to heal the land… so long as you humble yourself, repent and pray.

> *If my people, which are called by my name, shall humble themselves, and pray, and seek my face, and turn from their wicked ways; then will I hear from heaven, and will forgive their sin, and will heal their land.* (2 Corinthians 7:14).

So, we know the prophecy. But why did it come? I mean, one man burning incense to an idol would not destroy God's mercy that would last from generation to generation. As we continue to read the stories of the kings of Judah and Israel, we see it was more than just Jeroboam. This was a sickness that started generations before him. It really only takes one generation for the word to be lost. Can you believe that? But that's our reality. If you see the obvious connection to Christ and what He's about to do in His body and for His bride, you can put the book down and shout for a second. I'll wait… (praise break!).

Let's get back to Josiah and see how the prophecy unfolded. It's now the year 640 BCE, 330 years after Jeroboam and the high place prophet. God was considered "dead" in Jerusalem, and His word needed a resurrection in the hearts of His people—a people who had forgotten Him. What's worse, they buried the word in the temple. Here again, we see that pesky "madman" as he says, "What, after all, are these Churches now if they are not the tombs and sepulchers of God?"

2 Kings 22:3-13, loosely translated, tells us the story:

So Hilkiah, the high priest, says to Shaphan the scribe, "I found the Book of the Law in the house (temple) of the Lord." Hilkiah gives the book to Shaphan, and he reads it. Shaphan then goes to the king and brings the Book of the Law to him. He then says to the king, "Your servants have emptied out the money that was found in the temple and have placed it in the hands of workmen who have been appointed over the house of the Lord." Then he tells the king, "Oh, also Hilkiah, the priest gave me this book." Then Shaphan reads it to the king.

Now when the king heard the words of the Book of the Law, he tore his clothes (as a sign of repentance and grief). Then the king commanded Hilkiah the high priest, Ahikam the son of Shaphan, Achbor the son of Micaiah, Shaphan the scribe, and Asaiah, a servant of the king, said to them, "Go, inquire of the Lord God for my sake, for the sake of the people and for all Judah concerning the words of this book that has been found. (Go pray now.) For great is the wrath of the Lord, which has been kindled against us because our Fathers have not listened to and obeyed the words of this book. They, and we, have not done everything that is written concerning us.

Believe it or not, the word of God the king is referencing what was buried in the temple under a bunch of money. Is the word buried in you? What is covering it? What is piled atop of it? It is clear the priest in the temple valued wealth. What do you value over the word? It's time to clean out those rooms and the hidden places, time to open the windows and let the light in, time to uncover what the last king actually treasured... the word placed there. I tell you, there are Josiah's coming who will indeed look past the wealth that the Lord had given. Wealth is not a bad thing but a tool, but when the wealth has covered the word of God and has made it of no effect, the Lord will arise and remove all the wealth He gave you (Deuteronomy 8:18).

In this season, My children will act as Josiah's. They will tear their garments at the reading of the word of God and call for repentance, return back to the Father, and re-establish the word of God in them. Return to your first love, for God has said in John 14:15, *"If you love Me, keep My commandments."* Then the true throne of God can be established in the hearts of the Church as a whole and His people individually. This movement is already happening in Europe and other countries. It has even popped up in rock bands like Korn, who walks around the lobbies in their concerts, laying hands on the sick and leading people to Christ. Can we do any less to resurrect the word?

THE SEEKING OF OTHER GODS

The fulfillment of the Josiah prophecy came at a time when the nations of Israel and Judah were in a pretty terrible place. Every king before him, with very few exceptions, had turned away from the Lord in some way. Of the 39 kings who reigned after Solomon and the splitting of the Northern and Southern kingdoms, only a handful followed God and tried to do what was good and right in His sight. 1 & 2 Kings and 1 & 2 Chronicles along with many extra biblical sources tell us all we need to know about most of them. Both the Northern and Southern kingdoms were involved in the worship of other gods. Even Solomon, known as a man with great wealth and understanding, raised up high places and made treaties with other nations by marrying their daughters. As 1 Kings 11 tells us, He had 700 wives, who were princesses, and 300 concubines. And Solomon's wives turned away his heart. So, he was not wholly true to the LORD his God, like David his father. He went after Ashtoreth the goddess of the Sidonians, after Milcom the abomination of the Ammonites. He built high places for Chemosh, the abomination of Moab, and for Molech the abomination of the Ammonites on the mountain, east of Jerusalem. And so he did this for all his foreign wives, who made offerings and sacrificed to their gods.

Yes, he built the temple as instructed by the Lord, but he also built up altars to 700 false gods. Manasseh did what was displeasing to the Lord by following the practices of other nations, raising altars to Baal and rebuilding the shrines that his father Hezekiah had destroyed. He even sacrificed one of his sons in the fires of Molech worship. Hey! That's the same high place that Solomon established! He ruled longer than any king of Judah 698-642 BCE, 55 years, but his reign was only a reflection of those who had come before him. Is it any wonder that there is less than one chapter devoted to his reign? Would there have been an altar to Molech if Solomon had not raised high places for his wives? So, 233 years later, the kingdom is still repeating the same cycles and patterns of bringing these altars and high places into the House of God. King Ahab of Israel had done evil in the sight of the Lord. He married Jezebel, who killed God's prophets and built temples at Dan and Bethel. But wait, there's more!

In 2 Kings 1:2, we find Ahaziah seeking the council of Beelzebub. What was it that the Lord said to him? Is there no God in Israel that you would seek after Beelzebub? Ahaziah was clearly not seeking God first (Matthew 6:33). Otherwise, Ahaziah's healing would have been added to him. On and on, we read of the kings of Israel and Judah building high places, worshipping Beelzebub, Baal, Astaroth, and Meriketh. Repeatedly, we read that they did evil in the sight of the Lord. Here we see these generations who have sought after false gods (Exodus 20:3), *"You shall have no other gods before Me.*

Pop quiz: Were the kings corrupt because of the people, or vice versa? The people may have asked Saul to keep the choicest riches, but he also wanted them! (1 Samuel 15). These are God's (kings), and God's people, of whom He said that He would establish His name and throne in and with (2 Chronicles 6:6 and 1 Kings 5:5). The people He said His name would be glorified through. They built high places and planted gardens, even idols in the Holy place. In

God's house, there were male cult prostitutes (sodomites) in the house of the LORD (1 Kings 15:12). I wonder if anyone stopped to think, *This is going way too far here!* Let those who have ears hear the word of the Lord. What high places have been established in the Church over the years? What idols have we burned incense to?

Remember, these are not the effects of one generation. Israel, like us, had been sick for hundreds of years. And like us, we're always willing to throw away the word and go after other things. The Old Testament shows us a chronicle of Israel's repeated failure to obey God, and her refusal to keep His commandments. We teach from these passages but, honestly, are we any better? Jeremiah gives us God's thoughts on both Kingdoms, *"The children of Israel and the children of Judah have done only evil before Me from their youth."* (Jeremiah 32:30).

He delivered them from Egypt, yet they wanted to go back. "Send us a redeemer to deliver us! Remember your covenant, O' Lord!" Often this cry was sent up by a remnant. Oh, glory to God that He always keeps a remnant! And because of this remnant, He sends in the judges—Othniel, Ehud, Shamgar, Deborah, Gideon, Tola, Jair, Jephthah, Ibzan, Elon, Abdon, and Samson. However, after each one of them died, Israel goes right back! There are far too many Scriptures to quote concerning this, but study for yourself and you'll see. Give them Samuel; they'll cry out for a king—not rejecting him, but rejecting God (1 Samuel 8:7).

So we see it's not the man or king, or a prophet. Certainly not the pastor, the evangelist, the apostle, or the teacher that the people reject and put to death (Matthew 23:37) — it's God, and His word. Anyone who would kill the king's messenger would gladly kill the king. In contrast, people often embrace these very leaders instead of embracing God and His word. "Well, pastor, doctor, prophet, so and so says..." I don't care what they say. What does the word say? Is this not how many have been drawn astray by false doctrines? As Paul told Timothy, "Give yourself to reading, to exhortation, to doctrine" (1 Timothy 4:13). Give yourself to the word, so you can't be lied to or lead astray, so you can keep the words of His covenant.

What does the the psalmist tells us:

Israel does not keep the covenant of God; they refused to walk in His word and forgot the works and wonders He had shown them. How often they provoked Him in the wilderness and grieved Him in the desert. They tempted God and limited the Holy One of Israel. He parted seas and gave them manna from heaven, fire by night, and a cloud by day, but with all these signs and wonders, they still tested and provoked the Most High God. They did not keep His testimonies but turned back and acted unfaithfully like their fathers. See Psalm, 78:10-11, 40-42, 56-57.

Chapter 4

WAGES OF SIN

THE LITTLE THINGS

Ever since the Lord said, "And I will put enmity between you and the woman, and between your offspring and hers, he will crush your head and you will strike his heel," (Genesis 3:15-19). It has always been about killing the seed (the word) ... killing it at any cost.

I am a movie buff. I got my passion for cinema and theater from my mother. I believe they are fantastic ways of telling stories. I enjoy all types of films, comedy, action, adventure, and even some scary films. While I don't watch horror films like I used to. Mostly because the holy spirit won't let me. I believe there is a lesson to be learned in them. I do not subscribe to the idea that you should totally cut yourself off from the world in order to live a holy lifestyle (although a lack of holiness is another reason for the death of God in our age). One film that really speaks to me as I write this chapter is Stephen King's Pet Cemetery.

A Doctor and his family move to a rural town in Maine. One day, his daughter's cat dies and his neighbor buries the cat in an ancient cemetery. The cat comes back the very next day, but is changed for the worst. A little later in the movie, the little son of the doctor is hit by a truck and dies. The doctor, full of pain and grief, buries his son in that same ancient cemetery, even after he was warned not to do it. Well, the boy came back from the dead with the same evil spirit as the cat. One night, the neighbor, played brilliantly by Fred Gwynne, tells the doctor that he should never have taken him to bury the cat. The cemetery has a will of its own, and maybe it wanted the boy instead of the cat.

What is that old saying—it's the small foxes that spoil the vine. The father and the neighbor overlooked this small thing. The death of the cat was such a small thing that it seemed insignificant, but the father lost his son because he yielded to wickedness. In the end, he and the neighbor both lost their lives. It's the little issues that we tend to overlook. Oh, it's okay that the pastor is given to alcohol. Oh, it's okay that you are shacked up? It's okay that you watch pornography. It's okay—the Lord understands. God knows my heart. Yes, He knows it. He knows it's deceitful above all things, and desperately wicked (Jeremiah 17:9). What does the word of God say about a little leaven again (Galatians 5:9)?

One man said, "Before you take a wall down, you need to ask why it was there in the first place." The word of God is a wall of defense to the Church, and to a nation. But when you eliminate the word of God from the classroom of one generation, 1963, you eliminate it in the Church of the next generation. The enemy not only wants the word out of the schools, but he (satan) also wants it out of the Church. When the standard of the word is removed, all things become admissible. What is acceptable in the sight of the world is condemned in the sight of God. Do we not see that these small things are what the enemy is after? The enemy wants to use the bride to destroy the husbandman, for example, when Eve gave the fruit to Adam, Delilah paid by the Philistines to get Samson's secret, Jezebel and King Ahab, the 700 wives of Solomon, and Judas—intended to be a part of the Bride— who sold out Jesus for 30 pieces of silver. The person doesn't matter—it's the end game. For who is there to deliver the word to the nations now? How can they hear if they don't have anyone to teach them (Romans 10:14).

In war, a general may say, "It's okay to give up this little piece of land as long as we maintain the larger and more important piece." A doctor may remove a limb, so the patient does not die, but the Lord wants His body whole and in full working order. Yeah, you can function without your foot, but I'm sure you'd rather have it. You may think you're okay with the alcohol, with the lies, thievery, a little pride, a sprinkle of arrogance, a dash of will worship, or even a spoon full of adultery (fun fact adultery is also idolatrous worship, see Strong's H5003). But you may say, "I don't do any of those things. I follow the golden rule. I do unto others as I would have them do unto me. Just as long as I don't do the big things, or hurt anybody to the best of my definition of 'hurt.'" Right? Wrong! Beloved, we have all given up ground somewhere – see Romans 3:12. If the enemy gets an inch, he will take a mile. If he gains a bit of ground, he will go for the whole thing. The enemy couldn't care less about the little things people deem dismissive. The devil wants the heart of the Church. You may think, I'll lose a little ground here and gain more ground there, but this is faulty logic at best. This makes me think of Genesis 4:7, where God tells Cain, "If you do well, will you not be accepted? And if you do not do well, sin crouches at your door; its desire is for you but you must master it."

Sin is just sitting at the door waiting like a roaring lion, and it wants to master the *Church*, to sift us as wheat, even as it did Peter in Luke 22:31. Worry not, Jesus, our high priest, is praying and interceding for us always. Lucifer's anger, in part, stems from a place of pride, rejection, jealousy, and envy. The name Lucifer is translated from the Hebrew word *helel (*Strong's H1966), which means brightness. Before he abdicated his seat, his job was to directly attend to God. What a job description! The covering cherub (Ezekiel 28:11-19). Imagine standing before the Lord and reflecting His light—the light of Jesus, throughout heaven. Lucifer was covered in every precious stone, and he was a signet of perfection, full of wisdom and perfect in beauty. Lucifer saw the creation of man and felt that his position had been usurped like he had been demoted.

For what can truly represent and display the *honor* and glory of God but something that is like Him. We then, mankind, were always in God's plan, in Him and of Him before the foundation of the world (Ephesians 1:4). We have seen what happens to the proud when they think they are bad enough to take on the throne (Isaiah 14:12, Luke 10:18, and Revelation 12:7-17). He cannot defeat the Father. Lucifer could not exalt his throne, so he simply took the next best thing, the next acceptable substitute, the throne of the man... the little God who is made in God's image (Matthew 4:9 and Genesis 1:27).

Isaiah tells us that hell wishes to enlarge itself (Isaiah 5:14) "Therefore hell hath enlarged herself, and opened her mouth without measure: and their glory, and their multitude, and their pomp, and he that rejoiceth, shall descend into it."

Well, what does hell enlarge itself with? SOULS … it's taking ground.

When sin and death come on the scene, they are not small things. They want to expand themselves. Misery loves company. A virus has one goal, to multiply and copy itself, like that classic movie monster, the blob 1958. They are enemies that constantly come against the word of God and His children. To do what? Kill, steal, and destroy (John 10:10). Make no mistake; the enemy desires your soul. Death is not the devil here; it is a completely different foe. Sin and the devil (satan) are already defeated on the Cross.

The Bible tells us He spoiled principalities and powers, and made a mockery of them (Colossians 2:15). Jesus came to destroy the works of the devil (1 John 3:8). But death will be the last foe to be defeated (1 Corinthians 15:24-26). Death is not yet defeated and destroyed fully; otherwise, our bodies would not experience death and decay. It will only be defeated after the resurrection for those who enjoy the resurrection of eternal life . But death is under lock and key. It is controlled (Revelation 1:18). Jesus tells us that He holds the keys to death and Hades.

Glory to the Lamb that nothing is out of His control. As one man said, God's sovereignty knows no ambiguity. God uses death with the intent of resurrection. The enemy, satan, used it to bring separation from the destiny and purpose God has for His Church and us individually.

SYMPTOM OF SIN

By one man came sin (Romans 5:12). And with that, sin came death. Death is to sin as a high temperature is to sickness. Remember, sin is a thing, a spirit, and death is its symptoms—a death that continues to reign in the Church and in life because we would rather let the word die than we ourselves... cause meet effect.

We do not truly want to die. No, not really. See, the flesh wants to endure and will do whatever it needs to survive, including pray, repent, read the bible, worship, and bow, as long as it can rule and reign. We want the stuff we consider bad to die, but we never considered that even our human love is unacceptable to Him. But we're talking about the flesh here. No good thing in the flesh means just that, NO GOOD THING. That includes what we consider good things. If you're trying to save the good stuff, the bad stuff won't die. It'll just hold on. We cannot fix the flesh, nor can we make it better. God will make the flesh new, just as the spirit of man is born new in Christ Jesus. What is born of the flesh is flesh and what is born of the Spirit is spirit. One cannot remove the high places because we see that they are bad. We must remove the hidden things also. ALL of it must come down. Anything built by human hands must be cast away no matter how beautiful it looks.

This is why Christ says, take up your cross, and follow me (Matthew 16:24). This is why Paul says, "I have been crucified with Christ; it is no longer I who live, but Christ lives in me; and the *life* which I now live in the flesh I live by faith in the Son of God, who loved me and gave Himself for me" (Galatians 2:20).

We see that God always has a plan in place. Although He allows death to occur, even call for it, He would use death to bring about resurrection. After all, resurrection cannot happen unless death happens first (1 Corinthians 15:35). He spoke that life in the midst of a rebellious nation who ran after other gods like a swift camel in heat, but He still always spoke life (Jeremiah 2:23).

When Solomon, Jeroboam, Manasseh, Ahab, and Rehoboam all bowed their knees before idols, when each king did more evil than the kings that came before them and led the children of Israel and Judah to bow down as well, God sent a man. He sent a spirit, and that spirit (of Josiah) declared that the Lord Himself would heal.

Even those who did good in the sight of the Lord did not follow the Book of the Law. We read in 2 Kings 23:22, "Surely there was not held such a Passover from the days of the judges that judged Israel, nor in all the days of the kings of Israel, nor of the kings of Judah." Nobody got it right. Not one! From the days of Samuel the prophet, to the days of Josiah, no one got the Passover correct. I pose a question. If the Passover wasn't right, what else wasn't right? Indeed, all had turned aside together. They'd become corrupt. None does good, not even one.

Sin and death crouch at the door. But we must master it and subdue it. The Hebrew word for *subdue* is *Kabash* (Strong's H3533). It means to subject, subdue, force, keep under, bring into bondage. Just as God told Adam, Cain, and even Jeroboam, "If you will do as I command, you will be blessed. But if you do not, I will cut you off just as I did Solomon." What does sin, hell, and death want to do? Expand themselves, take territory, but you must master them—subdue them by the Spirit and the word. You have been given authority. Even in death, He still has a plan for resurrection, a plan for Josiah to come, a plan for healing, a plan to glorify Himself, His Son, and His people.

DECOMP AND BLOW FLIES

My first real encounter with death was on October 15, 2014. I received a phone call that changed my life. The day started out like any other day. I awoke and ran to film a version of Edgar Allen Poe's, *The Raven*. I went to the theater to do a performance of Radio Golf and finished up my night at a reading for a new project.

As we finished the reading, I made my way through the home to the restroom. Suddenly, my phone rang. I normally screen my calls, but I just felt like I had to answer. When I did, a heavy voice greeted me: "Hello, may I speak to Allen Maston, please?"

I was ready to say, "Place me on the do-not-call list," but I remained respectful. After all, I have worked at a phone bank and always hated rude people. So, I simply responded, "This is he. How can I help you?"

I remember being in a pretty joyful mood. I passed a few other crew members and greeted them. This, of course, was short-lived as the voice said, "Mr. Maston, my name is officer..."

I don't remember his name.

He continued, "I'm with the Phoenix Police Department."

Well, now you've got my attention. My ears perked up. I'll admit I was feeling a bit odd. I had never been in any real trouble—a few moving violations but nothing to justify a call at 10:30 p.m. "Hello, officer, how can I help you?" I asked, thinking it would be something like an emergency with my nieces, or something else that had happened before.

"Is your mother Candance Camphor McLemore?" he asked.

"Yes," I said. As I reached the foyer of the home, I paused just by the front door. My heart rate had elevated. I didn't even reach the bathroom. "Yes, that's my mom."

The officer asked for my mother's address. I responded as I stood still, "Yes, that is where she lives." Thinking there had perhaps been a fire or something, or maybe an accident. But the line of questioning began to get more and more odd.

Does anyone live with her?"

"No, just her," I replied. "I stay with her from time to time, just be around, but, no, it's just her in the home."

The officer said, "Hmm… does she sleep in the master bedroom?"

"Yes, officer. Where else would she sleep?" I chuckled slightly. "What's this about? Please just tell me my mom's okay."

He paused, took a breath, and said, "Well, sir, we found a body in the master bedroom."

You know, I do not envy officers of the law—men and women in public service who must report the worst of the worst news to people. I have officiated weddings, but I'm yet to preside over a funeral. I don't have the heart yet. The sound that escaped my mouth was something I could not repeat if I tried. In truth, I don't want to. I fell to my knees. I believe I fainted for a spell. When I came to, one of my castmates had my phone and I was on my knees apparently calling out to God. I remember one cast member, a big fellow we call Booker, laying hands on me and praying. They said I was speaking in a strange language. We know it as the heavenly language, *glossolalia, tongues*. It has not ceased. It's still functioning and I'm grateful because I had no idea what to pray in one of the darkest times in my life. I had nothing left. What came out of me was the Spirit of God and His holy language.

I spent the rest of the evening trying to reach out to my five siblings and family members— trying to get someone, anyone, to answer the phone or emails. No one answered. It showed how disconnected we were. My siblings and I eventually all got together and met at my mother's house. We had to break through the back door because no one had keys. The body had been removed after a month of sitting. Yes, my mother had passed a month before but was in the house for at least three to four weeks in the Arizona heat. Though the body was gone, the smell and spirit of death were still there. The responsibility fell to us as her children to clean and clear the home. My twin sister and I cleaned the master bedroom, where the body had been decomposing. It's a horrible sight to clean up the liquified purge of your mother's remains.

Imagine, if you will, a group of five adult siblings (minus my younger brother, Rashee), who had not seen or spoken to our mother in quite a long time. The last I'd spoken with my mother was a month prior. We had to come together and set things in order.

The body of Christ has been like this, a family coming together at an unexpected death, separated for decades and millennia. Obviously, tensions are high and some would rather air the dirty laundry of the other members in the family. "Where have you been?" "What about you?" All the blame-throwing and being divided over issues that are really not issues, unwilling to speak to one another. I believe Roberts Liardon once called it majoring in the minors. But now, there is a call to unite to come and clean up the mess and set things right.

Yes, we have been making a lot of noise, but has it been godly noise? Yes, we have looked good; we've actually never looked better. There are more Christian services in the world than ever before. But, alas, never less Jesus, never less word. Understand, just because one has the look of the anointing does not mean that power is moving. Just because there are lights and music does not mean God is in the room. As Kathryn Kuhlman once said, "Noise is not power." Noise is not life. In fact, what is dead can often look alive".

When a body dies, it makes a lot of noise. Hair and fingernails still grow, suggesting life when it is in fact dead. On the other hand, what has the fullness of life that can at times look dead Consider Jesus on the cross or Lazarus in the tomb. There is still life in the Church. Jesus has built it, and anything He builds endures. "And I also say to you that you are Peter, and on this rock, I will build My Church, and the gates of Hades shall not prevail against it" (Matthew 16:18). No matter how long it has lain in a tomb and looked dead, no matter how much it might stink, it's still alive. Unfortunately, the stench of death lingers and draws all sorts of vile creatures, vultures waiting to pick the bones clean, and blow flies waiting to nest and feed.

When my siblings and I finally walked into my mother's home, it was unmistakable, as nothing smells like a decomposing body, and nothing smells like death. The first thing you notice besides the smell, are blow flies. They're the first insect on the scene when flesh starts to decompose. They can smell it from up to a mile away according to some sources. Once they get there, they begin to eat, poop, and lay eggs. Did you know that the female can lay anywhere from 100-200 eggs in a sitting, and can lay up to 2,000 in her short life span? So, consider the math and one month of a decomposing corpse. Even if one fly came in one week, that fly could become two to four thousand flies. And they are enormous! I mean, unless you've ever seen one, you can't imagine how huge they really are. And the home was filled with them. Yeah, I hate flies.

This brings me to my point. While God cannot die, if He is neglected in our lives and out of the Church's, He will separate Himself. Ain't no "Son-shine" when He's gone. We are only alive because of His life. If the source of life is removed, death occurs. When the Lord and His word leave, it's a form of judgment. No God, no life (i.e., *death*). Does the word not tell us, if you do not keep all this law, then all these things will come upon you. For us, it is the law that is written on our hearts, the greatest law; loving the Lord God with all our mind, heart, soul and strength (Mark 12:28-31). We must see the parallels between Israel in the Ancient Near East and the Church today. Paul said these things were written for our example (1 Corinthians 10:11 and Romans 15:4). If we cannot learn from them, then we are worse than fools and deserve the curses that come to all those who deny Christ and the word of the Lord, curses that are outlined in Deuteronomy 28:15-68.

CURSED WITH A CURSE

WAGES OF SIN

Can you imagine? Your towns cursed. Your fields cursed. Your fruit baskets, and breadboards cursed. Your children, and your crops cursed. The offspring of your herds and flocks, cursed. Whatever you do, and wherever you go— you will be cursed.

It should be noted here that this is in addition to the curses in Genesis. These are just the effects of God not being there. He doesn't stop there though, oh no, He keeps going. He goes on to say, I myself, the Lord (He is going to do these things), I will send disaster, panic, frustration on everything you try to do until you are destroyed. You will be afflicted by pestilence, illnesses, diseases, famine, and such. The sky over your head shall be bronze, and the earth under you iron. It won't rain and nothing will grow. See Deuteronomy 28.

Suddenly, I hear my mother's voice shouting, "get over here and take this whoopin.' Don't make me come over there and collect you." There was nowhere to run from her discipline. Rain will turn to dust, you will be defeated and made an object of horror. Your corpses will be food for birds and wild animals. This means you will die in random places without a burial ceremony, and no one will frighten the animals away. No one will care what happens to you. The Lord will actively afflict you with physical and mental illnesses—the diseases of the Egyptians. You will stumble in the dark, blind leaders of the blind, unable to find your way. You will be abused and robbed, and no one will help you. Have you married a wife? She will be raped, or be taken by another man. Did you build a house? You won't live in it. Plant a vineyard; you won't enjoy it. Have an ox, it will be killed and you won't eat from its meat. Your donkey will be stolen, and you won't get it back. Your sheep, given to your enemies. Your sons and daughters, taken away and probably placed into slavery. Other people will eat the fruit of your labors. All this death and all these blow flies because Israel let the word of God die and did not heed His commands, and law. They didn't love Him, though they were married to Him.

Now let us consider Judah, the Church, the body of Christ and the one who was taken from His side. What are our blow flies, you ask? I mean, it's not like there are big gigantic fly-type creatures zipping around the spirit realm, vomiting, laying eggs, and causing all types of havoc, right? That would be crazy! Well, actually, yes, that's exactly what it's like. We call them principalities, powers, the rulers of the darkness of this world, spiritual wickedness in high places. Just like with Israel, we have an outline of what God will do to the people who forget His word. We will find it in Romans 1:18-29.

GOD'S WRATH REVEALED

The main idea for this entire passage is God's wrath against Godless nations who deny Him. This is obviously a curse—wrath revealed from heaven, sent from the throne. The scripture tells us that they (whoever these things come upon) have the wrath of God revealed from heaven against all of their unrighteousness and wickedness, those who suppress the truth about God. Some may ask, *what is truth*? And Pilate asked the same question (John 18:38). The truth is obvious and clear—it's been there since He said, "Let there be…."

Moreover, we who He no longer calls servants, but friends, can know His will (John 15:15), and have no excuse in denying His eternal power and divine nature. What greater evidence do we need than the cross and the resurrection? Now, although they claimed to be wise, saying they knew God, they did not glorify or give Him thanks. They became utile in their thinking, darkened in their foolish heart, and exchanged the glory of God for *idolatry*. These are people who knew Him, yet suppressed and held Him back. They did not give the fullness of the truth about Him.

Whose job is it to exalt Him among the nations? How many do we know who don't give the full counsel of God? Yet God will give them over to their desires for sin. As St. Augustine so eloquently said, "The punishment of sin is sin." There is a punishment for perversion, idolatry, and immorality. And that is more perversion, idolatry and immorality. The women exchange natural sexual relations for unnatural ones as do the men, burning with their lust for one another. These receive in themselves the penalty for their error (Romans 1:26-27). Do a quick Google search on the Churches that accept LGBTQ as righteousness and tell me that this is not the wrath of God upon a people who have killed His word. And exchanged the truth about God, for a lie. Worshipping the creation, instead of the Creator. They say to the tree, you are my father, and to the rock you gave me birth (Jeremiah 2:27). Evolution anyone? Do you see the point here?

We have unfortunately begun to hear and see a cross between the things of the true and living God and the things of this world, the body of Christ and the body of the wicked one. God has called the body of Christ to be separated and set apart. So, why are we seeing a mixture of the true and living God with witchcraft, astrology, false doctrine, idols, immorality, homosexuality, murder, perversion, lawlessness, all kinds of unrighteousness, covetousness, malice, gossips, slanderers, haters of God, insolent, arrogant, boastful, contrivers of all sorts of evil, disobedient to parents, senseless, covenant-breakers, heartless, and ruthless behavior.

Stop me if you haven't seen any of these in your life, or in your Church: I love the Lord God but thank the universe. I love the Lord God but I wonder what my horoscope says today. You cannot serve two masters. You must love one, and hate the other (Matthew 6:24). Ungodly tolerance to blatant sin, rejoicing in those who do them and are teaching others to do the same (Matthew 5:19). Making a mockery of the word of God, and God—Himself.

God will not dwell with a people who refuse to dwell with Him. The world is watching and, worse, so are our children. Complacency to the word is everywhere. How comfortable are demons sitting next to you? How comfortable are you next to them? A comparison of Romans 1:18-29 and Deuteronomy 28 is pretty clear.

God's wrath, albeit not the happiest topic, has been poured out and revealed first and foremost upon His people. Oh, stop trying to frighten us. That hell-fire and brimstone preaching went out 200 years ago!

We should be frightened… absolutely horrified. As we said earlier, it is a dreadful thing to fall into the hands of the living God (Hebrews 10:31).

Chapter 6

RALLY TO THE KING

PUTTING SIN TO DEATH

The previous sections took a strong look into the brazen laver to examine and clean ourselves with His word (Haggai 1:5,7 and 2 Corinthians 13:5). To truly sit and think on our ways and thus considered, to turn our feet unto His testimonies. For His word is a lamp unto our feet and a light unto our path (Psalm 119:105). Let us search and try our ways, and turn to the LORD… again (Psalm 119:59 Lamentations 3:40).

Up until now, I have pulled no punches. I have been heavy-handed and written as the Lord has led me. When I began this piece, He told me many would not agree, but I still had to write it. The effects of a dead word have gripped the body of Christ. Like in the days of Josiah, the word has been buried deep for centuries and needs to be uncovered. Unrighteousness must be uprooted. But you can't uproot it if you don't know how deep and far the roots go. This search can take time and be uncomfortable, like a deep cancer being treated. If you do not get it all, it can come back.

Scripture tells us not to let sin rule in our lives but to put it to death (Romans 8:12-13). Sin is defined by God as transgression, iniquity, and rebellion against His law (His revealed word) – I John 3:4. It is unrighteousness, that which is not in right standing with God (1 John 5:17). For one to sin, they have to know intuitively right from wrong, good from evil (James 4:17). Yes, sin is a thing, but it is also action, word, thoughts, and deeds. This understood, we see why we are still guilty. When we do something wrong, we have the ability to know good and evil. We have seen the result of the word dying and sin rising. When the word dies, His hand comes against us.

David learned this well. When given a choice, he decided to take the hand of the Lord rather than His hand being removed (1 Chronicles 7:17). Now that's something to think about—the hand and wrath of God against me. His judgment is only designed to bring me to repentance. It means that He still cares! When we were younger and our parents discipline us, they said, "We're doing this because we love you." But we didn't understand until we got older and had children of our own. He is still willing to discipline us because He cares. He chastens those He loves (Hebrews 12:6).

I don't want to be on the receiving end of God's wrath, but I've had my share of chastening. Let His word guide us, reveal our errors, and correct them. Let us teach our children to hunger and thirst after the word, doing what's right before the Lord lest the ship again veers away, and they wind up lost at sea. Any pilot will tell you, the smallest deviation off course will cause you to be miles and miles away from your destination. This is why Jesus called it the *narrow* path. Yes, He is a loving God. Yes, absolutely, He is love, but it does not change that He is also *wrath*. His wrath is also part of His character. The fear of the Lord is the beginning of wisdom (Proverbs 9:10 and Psalm 19:9). We would do well to remember the same God who blesses, can also destroy the soul in hell (Matthew 10:28). His wrath in Romans 1:18 is no different. If we receive it, see ourselves and be corrected, the word will be resurrected in our generation by a call from the King Himself… our King—"Rally to Me, to Me!"

RALLY TO THE KING. RESURRECTING THE WORD

The word "rally" means come together, to continue fighting after a defeat, or dispersion, so that the troupes may recover in health, spirits, or poise. Given everything we've discussed, I think we see a need here. Like the prodigal son coming to himself in the pigpen (Luke 15:11-32), we need to return home. The call has gone out from the King. "I want my bride back, My Church. Let all who stand with the Lord rally to me" (Exodus 32:26). Perhaps you know the idea by another term. For football fans, when your team is losing, all you can do is stand by and watch.

Coaches gather their team together at half-time and give a pep talk that sends them back out fighting. There's a game to be won. Coaches remind them that they're there to win. There are no wimps. As the saying goes, win or go home!

Consider any film you've ever seen that has a brilliant speech that summons the blood. William Wallace's shouting, "They may take our lives, but they may never take our freedom" sounds alot like Matthew 10:28. Don't fear those who can kill the body. When King Theoden says, "The horn of Helm Hammerhand will sound in the deep one last time," Gimli then blows a gigantic horn and they mount a glorious charge against the legions of Isengard. I see Nehemiah 4:20. Wherever you hear the sound of the trumpet, join us there! Our God will fight for us! One of my personal favorites is, "Once more unto the breach, dear friends, once more; Or close the wall up with our English dead," Henry V, Act 3 Scene 1 by William Shakespeare. I see all those monologues and movies are finally coming in handy. But honestly, this is a great speech. The whole point here is that it encourages them. And boy, do we love to be encouraged? To have someone tell us, go for it! You can do it! We spend a lot of time listening to motivational speeches or going to people to get motivated. The self-improvement industry made 9.9 billion in 2018.

The Lord wants to motivate and encourage His people because He is with us and will strengthen and uphold us with His right hand. Who sits at His right hand again? (Acts 7:55). So we should then encourage each other with that same encouragement (2 Corinthians 1:14). He wants to bring us to Himself as Elijah called all Israelites to Mount Caramel to witness the destruction of the prophets of Baal (1 Kings 18:19), to rally His troops as one.

We have known defeat, struggle, the wilds, and wilderness. We have known the sorrow and bondage of Egypt. We have had much speech and wise words, but they are of little value because the Kingdom of God is not in words, but in power (1 Corinthians 4:20). If there's no power, is the kingdom even there? If there is no power, the word of God seems to be dead. But rejoice, for it cannot be killed. His word is everlasting and stands forever. (Psalm 119:89 and 1 Peter 1:25).

It is time to rally to the King and resurrect the word!

UNTO THE GREAT CITY

We see the start of a spiritual rallying call in Nehemiah 8, showing us what happens when people, in our case, the Church, return to the word of God. The Jews had been released from their exile in Babylonia. The Temple at Jerusalem had been rebuilt, but Jerusalem was still open to attack. The people suffered on all sides from slavery to oppression, and to the destruction of their way of life. All these things, of course, are the fulfillment of the prophecy found in Jeremiah 25, showing us what happens when people are not careful to do all that is written therein (Joshua 1:8).

Nehemiah gets word that Jerusalem is *razed* to the ground. The walls are broken. Their defenses and boundaries are in ruin. With the city in such a disintegration, even if the refugees come home, they are vulnerable to attack. Learning of this, broke Nehemiah's heart. He mourned not only because of the condition of Jerusalem but because of the condition of the hearts of the people. Beaten soldiers whose courage hangs by a thread, need comfort and encouragement. It's a brokenness that needs mending and comfort. Well, Nehemiah's name happens to mean "Jehovah comforts." And through him and his generation, comfort came to the people. God sent out a rallying call to bring His people back to His word—back to Him. A revival brings back life and new hope!

I firmly believe that assuming Esther never married Xerxes, Nehemiah would not have had his ear. God is never without a plan (Jeremiah 29:11). Upon seeing his face, Xerxes asked Nehemiah, "What's wrong"? Nehemiah replied, "May the king live forever! Why should my face not look sad when the city where my ancestors are buried lies in ruins, and its gates have been destroyed by fire?" "What would you have me do for you?" Asks Xerxes. When people returned to the word, everything lined up for the word to work. Nehemiah asked the king for permission to return and rebuild the city. Xerxes sent him, the cupbearer, to Judah as governor, with one mission, to rebuild. The king even gave him letters explaining his support and provisions for timber from the king's forest. When we (the body of Christ) return to the word, the Lord will ask,

"What would you have me do for you?" Will we ask for wealth, favor, and fame or will we ask for understanding?

Let us remember that Jerusalem is the Church. And we see an important pattern here. Nehemiah had to recognize his sin. This caused reverence of the Lord to rise, and repentance followed. He rejoiced in the word of God, and even in the midst of his emotions, he was ready and willing to get to work. Let's watch.

> *4 And it came to pass, when I heard these words, that I sat down and wept, and mourned certain days, and fasted, and prayed before the God of heaven* (Nehemiah 1:4).

One only mourns what is dead or lost. He sees the issue. It is clear to him what the problem is, so the next thing Nehemiah does is reverence the God of heaven (and earth). He fasts and prays;

> *5 And said, I beseech thee, O Lord God of heaven, the great and terrible God, that keepeth covenant and mercy for them that love him and observe his commandments: 6 Let thine ear now be attentive, and thine eyes open, that thou mayest hear the prayer of thy servant, which I pray before thee now, day and night, for the children of Israel thy servants, and confess the sins of the children of Israel, which we have sinned against thee: both I and my father's house have sinned.* (Nehemiah 1:5-6).

Being before God, Nehemiah is faced with the realization of the sins of the Kingdom and of the people. So he repents.

He didn't blame others. He didn't say, "It's not my fault that the Church is in the condition it's in" or "I was born to this." Neither did Nehemiah say, "Why should I have to deal with this?" Instead, he mourns. His heart was broken and he asked God for forgiveness.

He then says,

> *11 "O Lord, I pray, please let Your ear be attentive to the prayer of Your servant, and to the prayer of Your servants who desire to fear Your name; and let Your servant prosper this day, I pray, and grant him mercy in the sight of this man." It was with this repentance that God showed compassion and granted him favor with the King* (Nehemiah 1:11).

Curious. He says *servant*, and then *servants*. He is not the only one in this there are others who think as he thinks and feel as he does. When a person or group of people who represent a nation turn to prayer and repentance, it always resets the game. It falls to us now, my brothers and sisters. To be a Nehemiah, Josiah, and Esther, prophets out of the east. To pick up the mantles where they have fallen, to clean the house, to rebuild the walls, and to restore the boundaries. We didn't cause this death. We didn't start the fire, but we are responsible for it. We are responsible for answering the call and responsible to repent before the Lord, not only our sins but the sins of our forefathers. To shout, rally to the King! He will hear our cry. He does not despise a contrite heart (Psalm 51:17). He exalts the humble (Matthew 23:12).

ALONG COMES A SPIDER

We must be leery as we continue, as we repent and rally to the word of God. Enemies are always at the gates, and sin waits at the door, desiring us. Just as God is doing marvelous work, along comes a spider, or even a snake. Nehemiah is introduced to these spiders in Sanballat and Tobiah. Though they made Nehemiah's job seemingly hard, the Lord was with him. Nehemiah defended Judah from the Samaritans, Ammonites, Arabs, and Philistines. With the Spirit of the Living God upon you, it never takes as long as you think. Even with the enemies at the gates hammering at you, He will return His people to His word; He will confirm His word with signs following. In 52 days, Nehemiah got the walls rebuilt, the Hananeel Tower, the Fish Gate, the Furnaces Tower, the Dung Gate in the South, the East Gate, and the gate beneath the Golden Gate in the East.

With the walls rebuilt, the word has returned, and Jerusalem looks the way it's supposed to. Suddenly, the people listened and responded to the word of God. They had been starving for the word. Well, you'd be starving also after 70 years. It has been a long time since the word had been delivered properly—universally, with power and authority, as it was intended to be. And the Church was unified under Jehovah *Nissi*.

God is now moving among them. Among His people, He has raised His *shofar* high and declared among the nations, "Rally to Me, to Me!" And the revival, the resurrection that follows, is the result of their response to the word of God. Let us rally to the King and return to Him, to His word, and to His ways. Fall in love again with Him and get to know Him. Sit at the Master's feet and receive His law. Be about His statutes, His precepts, and His commandments. Receive His word with gladness. His wisdom… is it not above all other wisdom? "[5] If any of you lacks wisdom, let him ask of God, who gives to all liberally and without reproach, and it will be given to him (Jeremiah 1:5-8). He does not withhold any good thing to those who are in the Lord (Psalm 84:11).

VISION OF THE OUTER COURT

As I was writing, a vision was given to me and I was instructed to add it to this book. There is a process to go from the outer court to the *holy of holies.*

I saw the tabernacle. I saw the *holy of holies* and it was filled with people upon people, upon people of every tribe and tongue, but there was no cloud over the mercy seat. There was no cloud of smoke in the *holy of holies.* Even the wings of the angels covering the mercy seat turned their backs to the people. And they, all of them, were led out of the *holy of holies.* The curtain that was torn was reformed. The center as the whole tabernacle shifted, moved backwards, and all the people were placed in the outer court toward the brazen laver and the brazen altar. One by one, all had to be cleaned by their own hands. Some cleaned their hands, some cleaned their eyes, but all cleaned their ears and members. One at a time, their candles were re-lit, and they were allowed back in the *holy of holies*. But others refused to be cleaned due to their children, spouses, and family. They chose not to be cleaned, and so, they all stayed in the outer court.

And the Lord said, "My Church stands before me with unwashed hands, filthy lips, and filthy ears, having heard and fed on doctrines of devils. They opened their bed wide and climbed into it with wickedness. They all have said yes. All have been false to me. Their candlesticks have been blown out. My presence has been hidden from them as they 'manufactured' strange fire before Me. Yes, they have all been false to Me in one way, shape, or form. But I will clean them up. I call them to repentance. To go back to the outer court to be cleaned! To be cleaned! To be cleaned! So that they may stand before Me as a great unit, as a great *legion*, as my bride without spot or wrinkle. Some will not come. Some will deny, reject, and renounce Me, saying, *I am clean. I don't need to be cleaned.* Woe unto those as the horn is blown! Those who will not be a part of Me, but joy unspeakable and full of glory to those who will; let them come and be rejoined to Me."

RALLY TO THE KING WITH PRAYER

There is a process to return to the word, as we saw from Nehemiah, Josiah, Manasseh, and any other occurrence where people had to return to the Lord. There is a process for resurrection—death, burial and then, do you see?

There is a process for getting back in the right place with Him. Some pray the Lord's prayer word for word, and while this is not a bad thing, I believe Jesus gives us a step-by-step approach. After this manner therefore, pray ye:

> *Our Father which art in heaven, hallowed be thy name* (Matthew 6:9).

We acknowledge, reverence, and worship His holy name. Giving the true and living God what is due before all creation, declaring before all, in heaven, earth and below the earth that He is God. He is worthy of His name, deity, and power and worthy of His Sovereignty. Has Christ not been given the name above every name? That'll preach.

> *Thy Kingdom come, thy will be done on earth as it is in heaven* (Matthew 6:10).

We acknowledge His authority and power over every principality, ruler, and dominion. We say that His kingdom has come and that every throne on earth must be removed and replaced with His throne, His will, and His way. Not only must it be done in heaven, but it must be done on earth. Are we not made of the earth?

> *Give us this day our daily bread* (Matthew 6:11).

We acknowledge that only He provides for our needs. But in saying this, we must remember that the word declares that man does not live by bread alone but by every word that proceedeth out of the mouth of God. So, give us this day your daily word to sustain, instruct, lead, and guide us in Your truth. Did Christ not tell us that His food is to do the will of Him who sent Him? We ask for He (Himself), who is the bread of Life.

> *And forgive us our debts, as we forgive our debtors* (Matthew 6:12).

This is all about repentance before the Lord, asking for His forgiveness as He sustains us. As His Spirit is upon us, it is a light that searches all our inner parts, showing us who we are. As we are led by the Spirit, we are led to repentance—repentance that is more than just weeping, repentance that is deep. If He has forgiven our debts (Oh wretched man that we are), how much more should we forgive others of their debts?

> *And lead us not into temptation, but deliver us from evil:* (Matthew 6:13).

> *For thine is the kingdom, and the power, and the glory, forever. Amen.*

It is the Lord who leads. He leads us into the work He has for us, into the destinies we are born for as He is leading us, whether it be into the wilderness or the mountaintop. Whether in war with the Philistines or giants, into pits of betrayal, prison, martyrdom, vats of boiling oil, or lions' dens, in every trial of every kind, we rejoice in the Lord who knows what awaits us there. Wherever You lead me, let me therefore, not fall into temptation. As the psalmist said, keep me as the apple of Your eye. In the wicked day, when fierce bulls of Bashan have hemmed me in, keep me from evil, from the shadow of death, and I will be kept.

RALLY TO THE KING WITH REVERENCE

I got my first Bible when I was about 12 years old. It was mine. I loved it so much; I even slept with it. I was so careful not to damage it, thinking it honored the word of God. I'm sure most of us have felt the same way. I even remember an old version of *Treasure Island*, where Black Dog the pirate tore a Bible. Even the other pirates thought it was a crime. Imagine that. While treating the book well because it's a book is a type of reverence. This is not what I mean when I say reverence. In fact, a worn Bible with torn pages, a missing cover, sticky notes, and highlighter markers show more reverence than a neatly kept one will any day. What's that saying? Someone with a Bible that's falling apart probably isn't. If someone invited you to the White House or 10 Downing Street, you wouldn't just show up any old way. No indeed, they would tell you what to wear. So why do we show up to the Lord any old way?

All throughout scripture, the Lord God tells us how to approach Him. Laws about purity, holiness, and worship tell us so much about Him and how to show proper reverence to the Most High God. The tabernacle is a great example of how to come before the true and living God. Before coming into the Holy of Holies, you *must* be cleansed at the outer court before coming into the inner court. Coming into the presence of the Lord without a proper bath is just stinky. You cannot approach a king any kind of way. And this is also not what you would call a sweet-smelling aroma to His nostrils. With that being said, cleanse and rid yourself of anything that has defiled your temple in any way (i.e., sin).

Reverence is an honor—respect so deeply felt it must be displayed from the inside out, not from the outside in. Otherwise, we have people who honor Him with their lips and not their hearts (Isaiah 29:13). God is always looking at the hearts of His people. Though there is a way we must carry ourselves, He is not concerned with how we look or what outfit we choose to put on for the day. It's our hearts He's after. "But the Lord said to Samuel, 'Do not look at his appearance or at his physical stature, because I have refused him. For the Lord does not see as man sees; for man looks at the outward appearance, but the Lord looks at the heart'" (1 Samuel 16:7). So our approach to our heavenly Father needs to come from a correct posture—he who has clean hands and a pure heart, Who has not lifted up his soul to an idol, nor sworn deceitfully (Psalm 24:4).

His angels cry, holy holy holy, the elders give Him glory, and the oceans applaud Him. All of creation declares His glory. Is He not worthy of such reverence? Is His word not worthy of it? He promises to give us one heart and a new spirit inside, removing the heart of stone and giving us a heart of flesh. In this new heart, He will write His law. Only then will He be our God, and we His people. Notice He says one heart, suggesting unity in Christ to come. This reverence is an automatic response of everyone who encounters Him. Let us encounter Him and see Him for the absolute wonder He is! Worship Him and adore Him. He is so worthy of being exalted and glorified. Let us approach Him as His sons before their great Father, in humility with fear and trembling, with clean hands and a pure heart, thirsty with faith, knowing He will give us *living* water to drink.

RALLY TO THE KING WITH RECOGNITION

One of my mentors used to say, "Sure, tell me anything," clearly expecting me to lie. You can lie to everyone else. You can even lie to yourself, and we do. Of course, that extra slice of cake won't be a problem for me. I can totally go to that place and not walk into sin. But you cannot lie to God. Ask Ananias and Sapphira (Acts 5). He literally sees and knows everything. Humble yourself before Him, knowing that He is right. His ways are right. His word is right. The Gospel of John tells us that if we say we have no sin, we deceive ourselves, and the truth is not in us. Sin only reveals where our weaknesses are. If we confess our sins, He is faithful and just to forgive us our sins and to cleanse us from all unrighteousness. If we say we have not sinned, we make Him a liar, and His word is not in us. In order to be convicted of sin, His word must first be in us.

If we confess, He will forgive. We see the first step to confession, then, is recognition. Indeed, if one does not know one is a sinner and does not know there is an issue, how can one repent? This is why acknowledgment is the first step. Conviction comes from the conscience, which is influenced by what it knows. That knowledge must be tempered by the Holy Spirit; else, the conviction becomes condemnation. This conviction and recognition go together like peas and carrots. It is the Holy Spirit that brings conviction. It is He who will prove the world to be wrong about sin, righteousness, and judgment (John 16:8). As the Holy Spirit speaks to you concerning the death of the word in your own life, you may feel guilt. That's good. It means the Holy Spirit is finally present in that area and something has to leave. The revealed will of God then creates the foundation for His law, breaking all other foundations, breaking the guilt. Surrender, bow, and yield yourself to the *Almighty.* Acknowledge where you have fallen short. See it, and repentance will follow.

RALLY TO THE KING WITH REPENTANCE

For without conviction, it is sin. We cannot talk about repentance enough, and its importance cannot be overstated. True repentance is a spirit, and is a gift of God. Repentance can only come from having a heart of repentance. Because of our sinful nature, repentance is undoubtedly necessary in order to be in right standing with God. Many times, we forfeit our blessings out of our rebellion and disobedience. God cannot dwell where there is sin. We cannot go before a Holy God dirty, without first repenting of our sins.

We must stop riding the "grace train." While His grace is sufficient in our weaknesses, you cannot afford to gamble with it. As the Scripture says, you shall not tempt the Lord your God (Deuteronomy 6:16). We ought to strive daily to walk in righteousness. For we are to be holy, for He is *Holy* (1 Peter 1:16). His grace and mercy extend to one end, to bring us back to Him. Repentance occurs when we have encountered His majesty at the throne in our most vulnerable state and have been exposed to His unfailing love, His uncompromising standard revealed in His word.

Many times, the scripture reminds us of the compassion He bestowed on many. Christ knew the hearts of men and women and expressed openly that their sins were forgiven (2 Samuel 12:13, Psalm 85:2, Isaiah 44:22, and Matthew 9:2). "Repent!" was the whole basis of Jesus' life (Mark 1:15). And if it was that high on Jesus' list, should it not be on ours? The body of Christ, as a whole unit, must repent. We must start anew so that God can fulfill His will for the Church. If people within the body of Christ are still in a state of brokenness with no healing, how then can we get the lost? God says, "Repent you, and I will save you – Acts 16:31. He would rather you repent and live than experience death (Ezekiel 18:23).

Repentance demands full confession and transparency. You must expose the enemy of your life in order to obtain peace and freedom. And the only way to be truly covered by Christ is to fully confess your sin(s). There is nothing hidden from God. Without repentance, freedom is hindered to the believer. But God desires His children to come out of the snares of the enemy. But you *are* a chosen generation, a royal priesthood, a holy nation, His own special people, that you may proclaim the praises of Him who called you out of darkness into His marvelous light (1 Peter 2:9).

You know that saying, "Tell the truth and shame the devil." We cannot be comfortable sitting next to demons. We (as a whole) should be so prayed up and filled with the word of God that there should be a "no vacancy" sign on us. God wants to fill us with holy things, not unholy things. Let us be His holy habitation. Jesus loves you. His desire is that all men and women not only obtain salvation (freely) but to return to Him. Having come this far, you must see where the word has died in you. So repent, my beloved, and believe the gospel of Jesus Christ again.

RALLY TO THE KING WITH REJOICING

Why did David dance out of his clothes? Because the Ark of the Covenant returned to Jerusalem! 2 Samuel 6 and Deuteronomy 16:11 tell us, you shall rejoice before the LORD your God; you, your sons and daughters, your male and female servants, and the Levite who is in your town. Also, the stranger, the orphan and the widow who are in your midst in the place where the LORD your God chooses to establish His name. He has established His name and His word in you. So praise the Lord all ye nations! Jump, shout, holler, and party! There are those who will speak against this saying victory is not in praise but in Jesus. In fact, both are true. He abides in our praises (Psalm 22:3). So, victory is in praise as long as Jesus is in it. You should always have something to rejoice over. The Lord has arisen in your heart. He has forgiven you and placed you back in a positive position.

Who is this wonderful God who has saved and redeemed us with His blood? The Lord Jehovah is His name. You who have turned back to Him and have been forgiven of Him, welcome home. Therefore, be filled with joy. Rejoice, has He not made you glad? (Psalm 92:4). The joy in the home of the prodigal son's family was high. The fatted calf was killed. The party went on all night long because of his awaited return. Even the angels rejoice in your return (Luke 15:10)—joy unspeakable joy, and full of glory! So rejoice in the Lord always: and again I say, rejoice (Philippians 4:4-8). This is a celebration! And should we not celebrate? He is our exceeding great reward (Genesis 15:1). He is our inheritance and portion (Numbers 18:20 and Ezekiel 44:28). Lift up your heads and be lifted and the King of Glory shall come in (Psalm 24:7). Enter His gates with thanksgiving and into His courts with praise (Psalm 100:4).

But, what if I didn't feel like doing any of this? What if I'm depressed? What if I'm angry or reminded of my sin? What if my denomination says we can't dance, or sing or party at church. What if I'm Batman? What if the moon is made of cheese? The way you feel has nothing to do with the price of tea in China. We walk by faith, not feelings—By the word, not by wounds. If we are truly to be Spirit-led people and sons of God. For all those who are led by the Spirit are the sons of God (Romans 8:14), then our emotions cannot rule or lead us. We rejoice because we know His word supersedes our feelings. It supersedes our circumstances. His word is the final authority. He is not a man that He should lie, nor is there a shadow of turning within Him (James 1:17). Remember, your words create your world and your atmosphere. Who's better at making worlds than He? So let's make His word ours (John 12:49).

Rejoice, *sâmach chairō*, (Strong's H8055 and G6463), means to brighten up, to be full of glee, to cheer up, make glad, to make very merry (English, Hebrew, Greek definitions).The idea is to make yourself glad...again. Something will always try to interfere and give you a reason not to be glad, but to this, the psalmist says, "Bless the Lord oh my soul and forget not his benefits" Psalm 103:1, "for He has made you glad" and Psalm 92:4. If your joy is found in Him, there is no reason not to rejoice.

Dr. Howard Bell is one of the most joyful people I know. He is a *quadriplegic*. This man of God is always singing and worshipping God. Like, always. He is quick to stop in the middle of a conversation and say, "Can we just worship for a minute?" He never hesitates. Lost your job, rejoice! Sick, rejoice! Car stolen, rejoice! dry and barren land rejoice. Every situation is cause to rejoice. Knowing this, that in this world, you will face trouble, but take heart for Jesus—The Word, has overcome the world (John 16:33).

When you pass through the waters, He is with you always. The rivers shall not overflow or overtake you. But in His faithfulness and lovingkindness, He is there with you. If (you) ascend into heaven, He is there; make your bed in hell, yep He's there also (Psalm 139:8). When you walk through the fire, and you're going to, you won't be burned. Neither shall the flame touch you (Isaiah 43:2). The enemy comes in like a flood and God raises up a standard (Isaiah 59:19). He who saved you is able to sustain you with His JOY and life. So, rejoice. Your afflictions may be many (Psalm 34:19). But David said, "Had I never been afflicted, I never would have learned your statues" (Psalm 119:71). A statute is the written and spoken word, His law, and this law says rejoice in HIM. And again, I say rejoice!

RALLY TO THE KING WITH WORK

We need to see an increase of servitude in the body of Christ. It's not that people aren't serving, but it's not as widespread as it should be. Let's be honest… Most people in the body of Christ aren't moving to serve in their local Church. If all the faculties of your body were not in top working order all working together doing their job it means you're sick, your body won't function properly. Should we be sitting on our butts in service, getting fat and lazy like the humans in the movie *Wall-E*? There is work to be done for the Kingdom of God. And God hates slothfulness (Proverbs 6:6; 19:15; Ecclesiastes 10:18).

Each of us has received some gifts from Him (Ephesians 4:8). He places those gifts in the Church as He desires, giving us all some job or public function to fulfill. Casting out devils, speaking with new tongues, laying hands on the sick, saying to this mountain, "Be removed and cast into the sea," and greater works. These signs shall follow those who believe (Mark 16:17-18). Follow means "to go" or come after. For signs to follow, you must take your gifts and GET TO WORK. He does not desire that we spend all our time on prayer and Bible study, conference hopping, getting spiritually fat and feasting on the word, yet giving nothing out. Are you sharing the word of God with others? Are you allowing God to use you for a testimony? Are you out in your local community, contending for the faith? Are you being a light on your job for others? Does your family know about the true and living God you serve? God has commissioned us to share the Good News of Christ with others (Matthew 28:19).

After Jesus sent them, the apostles went out and they began to work. The Holy Spirit worked with and confirmed the word (Mark 16:20). Not them. Not their gifts, but the Holy Spirit confirms the word. You have an assignment. You have a word, and it's not to sit on your "duff"... it's to GET TO WORK. The Great Commission is a job description. It's marching orders. While on the job, the full resources of the Kingdom are at your disposal. One of the first people to call an airstrike was Elijah. The Kingdom is revealed in power. The continuing flow of His power requires that we— GET TO WORK.

Discernment, tongues, interpretation, prayer, fasting, prophecy, faith, wisdom, knowledge, healing, miracles, and the word of God. All these gifts are the weapons of our warfare. They are used for combat against the wicked one. We are not fighting a natural battle—it's a spiritual battle. To defeat the enemy in our lives and have the victory over the opposition, we must learn how to counter-attack the battles and trials we face every day, just as a sniper who is positioned in a high place aims low. These weapons are your bullets. They are our Kung-fu and they are strong. What are we doing with what He died for?

Many of us are waiting for someone in authority to give us the okay, to say you're ready to go only after you've gone through seminary school, training, and the official ordination of man. Don't wait until after you've been thoroughly vetted. While I agree with the steps of education and proper theological training, there is a godly protocol and order. In some places, you should sit down and wait for the person in authority to bring you up. But who has more authority than the Lord? When I traveled for ministry in Belgium, France, and Kenya, I didn't need man's approval. I and those with me, went because we were sent by the Lord. The King signed off on our mission. And guess what, signs followed because we GOT TO WORK.

In 1933, the great General Lester Sumrall told the story of

when he was told to "go." It was in the middle of a revival that was supposed to last for some days. Right in the middle of it, the Lord told him to leave and go to a place he had never been. He gave plenty of excuses, but the Lord replied to them, "I said Go." So, General Lester sold his car and went. The result was a wonderful connection with Howard Carter that took him around the world to over 100 nations and birthed the ministry to one of the greatest apostolic evangelists of the 20th century. I don't have the education—GO. I don't have any money—Get going. I don't have the training. Will you go? I don't know anybody—I SAID GO. God is not interested in our excuses. He is looking for a willing vessel that will say, "Lord, here I am, send me." When we are about our Father's business, He then will be about ours.

Moses had the same excuses, so did Abraham, so did Gideon… Heck, so did I. We are all given the same answer. Basically—"Didn't I already tell you to go get to work?" When it is the Lord sending you, He will make the provisions as you go. As you put your hand to the plow and get to work, you need no one to send you. I've already sent you. Who gave Paul the okay to go? Who gave Abraham the okay to go? Who sent Moses to Pharaoh? Who sent David to slay Goliath of Gath? Who sent John the Baptist? Who sent Christ into the wilderness? Was it not the Lord of all?

If He has said it, that sets it. Have you been commissioned to go by the Lord? Have you received a burden for something? When Josiah heard the word read to him, for it had been hidden, he tore his clothes and repented and got to work. Nehemiah just heard of the condition of Jerusalem and got a burden for it. As soon as the king asked Nehemiah what was wrong, the Holy Spirit began talking. "Sir, if it's alright with you, please send me back to my home, send me to Judah, to the city of my fathers' tombs, that I may rebuild it." (Nehemiah 2:5).

I shared in the beginning that I got the burden for this book over four years ago, and yet I waited for someone to send me, not realizing I was already sent. I trust I'm not too late, and its words are still relevant. Beloved, if God has stirred a fire in you, then go to work. If it breaks your heart, then go to work. You're ready. Go Go Go and spread the word that has been placed in your mouth. The Holy Spirit will work with you and confirm the words. If this is you, go to work… I implore you— Go.

CONCLUSION

Those who came before us made mistakes… can't help that. They gave us what they were given. Will we make the word live for those who come after us? God thinks generationally, will we? It is our job to "Rally to Him," so He can resurrect His word, and through it, the power of the Holy Spirit. We may stand as an example of Christ, yet not we, but Christ in us. Let the word live in you, Beloved. For if it is not alive in you, the Holy Spirit has nothing to work with, or confirm.

We are being called upon as Nehemiah's and Josiah's in this day, to rebuild, heal, comfort, and defend the boundaries, to remove what is unholy from the Holy place and call the people back to righteousness. To unite the people under their one true King, to show them that their beautiful city is rebuilt, and to build the altar again. There are still holdouts waiting in the body, waiting for the promise of God, waiting for an outpouring of the Spirit that will be greater than any before. There are people like Anna who will not leave the temple, but worship night and day, fasting and praying, even as the psalmist sang, "I will wait for the LORD, my soul does wait, and in His word do I hope." For He has sent someone to call a rally to the King!

Oh, how beautiful are the feet of them that preach the gospel of peace (the Good News of the word of God), and bring glad tidings of good things. Return to the word, O' Judah. Will it be us who sends up the cry, or will we pass this over to the next generation? Will we resurrect the word and ways of God, or will we be distracted by other things? Let us put away those things that have so easily beset our elders and ourselves. Repent of the wickedness of our hearts and mindsets. Repent of the sins of those who have come before us. Not that our repentance can forgive them, but their lives, their habits, and altars built. We must call fire down upon those wicked altars.

Will you join me in a prayer of repentance? Not only for the Church but for you and your family. We must ask the Lord to resurrect His word and life within us. Ask Him to remove the high places and destroy the altars and establish His throne upon our hearts. King Manasseh was considered the worst King in the history of Israel or Judah, but in the end, He repented before the Lord. God used Manasseh to begin the destruction of altars and high places he had a hand in raising. Beloved, it does not matter what you've done, or what you worshipped at, or how long the altar had been raised up. The Lord will take you back and He will use you to resurrect the word in your life, your family, your local Church, and your community.

CLOSING PRAYER

Blessed are You *Adonai,* King eternal. Your light divides the day from the night and makes the shadow of death as bright as the morning: Incline Your ear to us, Lord. We yield our hearts to You. Father, your word says in 1 John 1:9, "If we confess our sins, You are faithful and just to forgive us and to cleanse us from all *unrighteousness.*" And we have sinned—not against man but against Your word. We have known it, and not obeyed, Heard it, and not headed. We have held our tongue when You bid us to speak and sat down when You told us to stand. We have accepted and taught wicked doctrines. We have broken Your covenant, and built altars to more idols than we can count.

But You, O Lord, are the perfect keeper of the covenant for Your great name's sake. Look upon Your children now and cleanse us with Your love and grace. Be zealous over us again as we throw ourselves upon Your mercy. We place our will upon Your altar and sacrifice them there. Cleanse this temple and take Your rightful place as Lord, Husbandman, Captain, King, and God. For who can remove these high places, but You. Thank You, Lord, for Your love and grace. For separating us from the altars and curses of the past. Rain Your fire down upon them—that they may not stand. Fill us, O Lord, with You, and only You, that we may unite in You as one body, a bride without spot or wrinkle. Now bless us, Lord. Keep us. Let Your spirit shine upon us. Be gracious to us and give us peace. Amen.

THE WORD IS ALIVE IN ME

Father, You are my refuge and my shield. I put my hope in Your breathed word that is alive and living in me. Your word is a lamp for my feet and a light to my path. I have ears to hear it. Your word judges my thoughts and the attitudes of my heart. It's active, daily, dividing my soul and spirit, joints, and marrow like the high priests of the tribe of Levi. You are my High Priest.

I carry the glory of the Lord within me. I stay on the path of purity, and I live according to Your word. I hear the word of God and obey it. And so I am blessed above all nations because I keep His word before my eyes. My way is made prosperous and I have good success. The grass may wither and the flowers will fall. Heaven and earth will pass away, but your word will never pass away. The word of my God endures forever within me.

His word was always in the beginning with Him. It is Him. It's flawless. It shields me. I take refuge in it. He unfolds it to me. The mysteries of His word are revealed and given without measure. It gives me hope. It brings me life, light, and understanding. Let us delight in the meat of His word and making merry in the things that are bestowed in His promises. Let us delight and be joyful in the wisdom of God's provisions. Others may be secure in their inventions and in their wealth that they cannot take with them. But my delight is ever in the word of the Lord. I am assured and sustained by every word that proceeds out of the mouth of God, that it brings faith, hope, and unconditional love for me.

Let the word of God remain in me, for it will not return void but will accomplish what He desires it to achieve for the purpose of His Will. None of Your words will be delayed any longer in me but will spring forth great things in a new season. Whatever You say will be fulfilled for Your glory. You are Sovereign, Lord. For all His words are true. All of His righteous laws are eternal. My whole being waits and hopes in Your word. I trust, lean, and rely on it. It is good for me not to lean to my own understanding. For what is understanding? What is wisdom, if not from the Lord? Your word, Lord, is life to my marrow and bones. I have hidden it in my heart that I might not sin against You. I am His child. I turn my ear to His words. I pay close attention to what He says and do not let it out of my sight. I meditate on it day and night.

Write Your word on the tablets of my heart, and the words of Your covenant. You have made me a good land. You've given me a heart of flesh and placed Your Spirit within me. No ravens will remove the seed of Your word. It will not fall upon stony ground because You have already cleansed me with Your word. You spoke it and it has healed, delivered, and rescued me from hell, death, and the grave.

I am not ashamed, for I have rightly divided Your word and yielded myself to it. Yes, You are the Living word that is alive in me, keeping and sustaining me because of Your word. I am seated in *heavenly* places and cannot be removed. Your word endures forever. Let thanksgiving, glory, honor, dominion, power, and might be unto You, my Lord, forever and ever. In Jesus' matchless name. AMEN.

To God be the Glory in all things.

May the Lord Christ Jesus be with you all in His service, Allen Maston.

APPENDIX A

As it has been the basis for the seed of the idea planted *via* the Holy Spirit. I felt it needful to include a copy of Nietzsche's parable at the end of this writing that one may have the full outline of the idea presented by Nietzsche.

The English translation

THE MADMAN—Have you not heard of that madman who lit a lantern in the bright morning hours, ran to the marketplace, and cried incessantly: "I seek God! I seek God!"—As many of those who did not believe in God were standing around just then, he provoked much laughter. Has he got lost? asked one. Did he lose his way like a child? asked another. Or is he hiding? Is he afraid of us? Has he gone on a voyage? emigrated?—Thus they yelled and laughed.

The madman jumped into their midst and pierced them

with his eyes. "Whither is God?" he cried; "I will tell you. We have killed him—you and I. All of us are his murderers. But how did we do this? How could we drink up the sea? Who gave us the sponge to wipe away the entire horizon? What were we doing when we unchained this earth from its sun? Whither is it moving now? Whither are we moving? Away from all suns? Are we not plunging continually? Backward, sideward, forward, in all directions? Is there still any up or down? Are we not straying, as through an infinite nothing? Do we not feel the breath of empty space? Has it not become colder? Is not night continually closing in on us? Do we not need to light lanterns in the morning? Do we hear nothing as yet of the noise of the gravediggers who are burying God? Do we smell nothing as yet of the divine decomposition? Gods, too, decompose. God is dead. God remains dead. And we have killed him.

"How shall we comfort ourselves, the murderers of all murderers? What was holiest and mightiest of all that the world has yet owned has bled to death under our knives: who will wipe this blood off us? What water is there for us to clean ourselves? What festivals of atonement, what sacred games shall we have to invent? Is not the greatness of this deed too great for us? Must we ourselves not become gods simply to appear worthy of it? There has never been a greater deed; and whoever is born after us—for the sake of this deed he will belong to a higher history than all history hitherto."

Here the madman fell silent and looked again at his listeners; and they, too, were silent and stared at him in astonishment. At last he threw his lantern on the ground, and it broke into pieces and went out. "I have come too early," he said then; "my time is not yet. This tremendous event is still on its way, still wandering; it has not yet reached the ears of men. Lightning and thunder require time; the light of the stars requires time; deeds, though done, still require time to be seen and heard. This deed is still more distant from them than most distant stars—and yet they have done it themselves.

It has been related further that on the same day the madman forced his way into several Churches and there struck up his requiem aeternam deo. Led out and called to account, he is said always to have replied nothing but: "What after all are these Churches now if they are not the tombs and sepulchers of God?"

Source: Friedrich Nietzsche, The Gay Science (1882, 1887) para. 125; Walter Kaufmann ed. (New York: Vintage, 1974), [pp.181-82.]